PERIYA PURANAM

Amenity is He who is rare to be comprehended
And expressed in words by all in the worlds
In His crest rest the crescent and the flood
He dances in Ambalam
We hail and adore His ankeleted flower feet.
Periya Puranam

PERIYA PURANAM

V.V.S. Manian MBA
Dr. Nartana Karthikeyan PhD

AAYU PUBLICATIONS
New Delhi-110086

Cataloging in Publication Data--DK
Courtesy: D.K. Agencies (P) Ltd. <docinfo@dkagencies.com>

Manian, V. V. S., 1939- **author.**
Periya Puranam / V.V.S. Manian, Dr. Nartana Karthikeyan. -- First edition.
pages cm
Includes bibliographical references.
ISBN 9789391685140

1. Nayanars--India--Tamil Nadu--Biography. 2. Śaivism--India--Tamil Nadu--History. I. Cēkkiḻār, active 12th century. Periyapurāṇam. II. Karthikeyan, Nartana, 1980- author. III. Title.

LCC BL1280.59.M36 2021 | DDC 294.551309225482 23

Published by:

AAYU PUBLICATIONS
D-134, Agar Nagar, Prem Nagar-III
New Delhi-110086
Tel: 09910728725, 09654504227
Email: aayupublication@gmail.com
www.aayupublications.com

Periya Puranam

First Edition 2022

ISBN: 978-93-91685-14-0

PRINTED IN INDIA

Printed at Unitech Graphic Point, Delhi

TRINITY MIRROR
NATIONAL ENGLISH DAILY FOR THE PEOPLE

MAKKAL KURAL
NATIONAL TAMIL DAILY (Since 1973)
(VOICE OF THE PEOPLE)

FOUNDER EDITOR : M.S.

Taste Tamil culture, soak in bakthi in this treatise by VVS Manian

The great epic "Periyapuranam" is a literary fountain, flood of devotion and a vast sea of love. It is called "the supreme star" in the galaxy of Tamil literature.

This book now in your hands is actually an in depth treatise on Periyapuranam by Mr VVS Manian, a veteran columnist with over 50 years of writing experience.

This is an extremely valuable book on the theme "Saivism" which is the oldest and cherished philosophical system of Hindus which highlights the glory of Lord Shiva and clarifies many pressing questions in our mind.

To show their utmost devotion to Lord Shiva, the 63 Nayanmars have sung hymns, drenched in divinity and love for the god. They saw the Lord as master, bridegroom, friend, father, mother, kinsman and protector. He is all things that the poet-devotees cherish in this transient world. Periyapuranam not only narrates the tales of such devotees, also dwells on issues like women empowerment and rights how women empowerment was considered important. The reputation of Ilayankudi Mara Nayanar can be cited as an example.

It also glorifies three women religious followers known as Isaiganiyar, Karaikkal Ammaiyar and Mangayarkarasiar. Sekkizhar popularized the 63 Nayanmar saints by rendering their lives poetically in 'Periya Puranam'. It is a masterpiece in literature, history and music.

Devotion to Shiva takes many forms in the Nayanmars ecstatic outpourings. Sambandar and Sundarar are the foremost of the Nayanmars, describing the cosmic nature of the Lord frequently in their songs.

This book surely evokes an new interest to understand the various aspects in this great epic.

The learned author expounds the subject in very great detail and tries to present the lives of the 63 saints in a very easy to understand simple language.

In addition the book also has a detailed chapter on cosmic dance of Lord Nataraja aptly quoting Dr. Nartana Karthikeyan a scholarly researcher on Bharatanatyam.

Cosmic dance and Lord Nataraja have been featured in most of the Tamil literatures including in divine Thirumurai.

To reach out to various section of readers, Mr.Manian has published the prose rendering of this work written in Tamil, in English.

The layout and some of the drawings on the lives of the Saiva Saints in this book was done by the author himself.

The life of the 63 Nayanmars has already appeared in the evening English daily "Trinity Mirror" in 2015-2016 as a weekly feature article.

I am sure reading the book will give the reader a taste of ancient Tamil culture soaked in bakthi leading to a rejuvenated faith in Hinduism.

R Muthu Kumar
Editor, Publisher
Makkal Kural
Trinity Mirror

MEMBER INS

Chennai - #1, First Main Road, United India Colony, Kodambakkam, Chennai - 600 024.
Phone : +91-44-2473 3900 / 2473 3910 Fax : +91-44-2473 5700, 2473 2700
E-mail : makkalkural@gmail.com / trinitymirror1@gmail.com
Website : www.makkalkural.net / www.trinitymirror.net.

Pray Shiva, Shiva-the bliss of Shiva is attained

Thirumular

Periapuranam is a great Tamil literary work. The puranam explores in detail the life of the sixty three saints or nayanmars as they were popularly called . These saints hail from all castes, the low and the high. The life of each saint is a grand illustration of how immense faith in God relieves moral sufferings, pain and makes one enlightened.

Periapuranam has immense influence over the devotional tradition of Saivism in South India. Periya Puranam is the twelfth "Thirumurai". The epic was written during the reign of Kulothunga Chozhan II (AD 1113-1150). Sekkizhar who was the prime minister in the Chola Court had access to innumerable historic evidences such as writings on stones, sculptures, copper plates, etc. The divine epic "Periya Puranam" is the story of Nayanmars who adored Lord Shiva and spent their entire life chanting "Om Namashivaya".

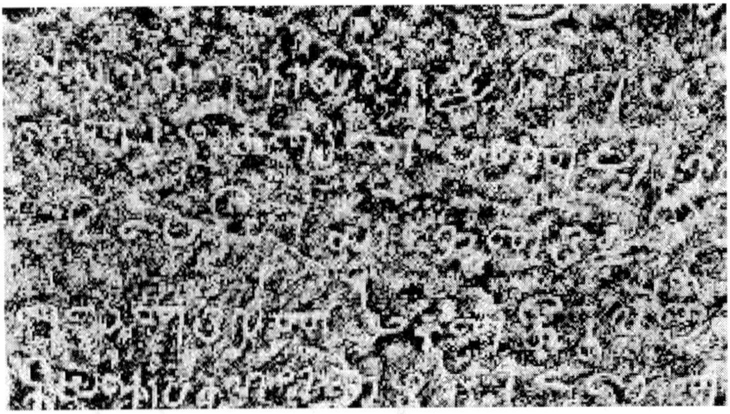

Stone inscriptions

CONTENTS

1

ADIPATHTHAR NAYANAR

Adipatthar lived in Nagapattinam. He was a very staunch devotee of Lord Shiva. He was the head of a group called Paradhvar. The main source of income and food for them are the fish got from the sea. Adipatthar used to toss to the sea the first catch of fish to the God. He will follow this act of providing fish to god even on days when he happened to catch only one fish. He will starve the whole day with happiness. God decided to test his devotion, love and patience. Many consecutive days, he caught only one fish which he happily threw it in the sea. He endured starvation with satisfaction. One day, he got a golden fish with rare gems. Without a moment hesitation, he gave it to god.

The Lord who was watching Adipatthar descended from the sky and blessed him and his people saying "all of you people be with me forever. Adipatthar attained place near God himself.

2

AIYADIKAL KADAVARKONE NAYANAR

Pallva King Aiyadigal Kadavarkone was a ruler of the Pallava dynasty and was ruling from Kanchipuram. Later he became the 46th Nayanar.

Kanchi, thc capital of the Pallavas is known as the city of active power. Located on the banks of the Vegavathy River, Kanchipuram has been ruled by the Pallavas, the Medieval Cholas, the later Cholas, the Later Pandyas, the Vijyanagar Empire the Carnatic Kingdom and the British. In Hindu theology, Kanchipuram is one of the seven Indian cities to reach final attainment. The city is a holy pilgrimage site for both Saivites and Vaishnavaites.

The king Aiyadigal Kadavarkone worshipped Shiva with faith and devotion and ruled his kingdom with his royal stick of justice i.e., the Justice of Shiva. As a brave warrior and courageous king, he protected the Shiva and Hindu temples and infused the spirit of Saivism into his subjects. The king was fluent in Tamil and Sanskrit languages. His knowledge of Tamil and Sanskrit has been the source of his Tamil hymns on Shiva.

The king felt the royal crown was a hurdle in serving the Lord and singing His fame. He gave the royal throne to his son and set off to serve the Lord. He went to the abodes of the Lord, who has Moon as an ornament over His golden matted hair and sang a Venpa (Tami poetry).

The king went to Chidambaram, saluted, and offered a lovely Venpa in praise of Nat raja, the cosmic dancer. After spending few days in Chidambaram, he proceeded to holy places worshipping Shiva. He continued his pilgrimage to innumerous abodes of the Lord and did his service singing the hymn to God. His salutations went on for a long time and he reached the land of Lord Shiva.

Kanchipuram

The Nayanar composed Kshetra Tiruvenba. It was composed by him when he visited many sacred shrines of Shiva in different places. The composition was very big and only24 are surviving. Using these 24 poems, Shekkizar composed his life history in Periyapuranam. This Kshetras Thiruvenba is a part of 11th Thirumurai.

Kailasanathan Temple

The demon under Nataraja's feet signifies that ignorance is under his feet
The Fire in this hand (power of destruction) means destroyer of evil
The raised hand signifies that he is the savior of all life.
The Ring at the back signifies the cosmos.
The drum in his hand signifies the origin of Life

Nataraja Temple, Chidambaram

3

AMARANITHI NAYANAR

Thou to me art parents, Lord
Thou all kinsmen that I need
Thou to me art loved ones fair
Thou art treasure rich indeed
Family, friends, home art Thou
Life and joy, I draw from Thee
False words good by Thee I leave
Gold, pearl, wealth art thou to me
Hymn of Thirunavavukarasar

In the Chola kingdom there was a picturesque village known as Pazhaiarai on the banks of the river Cauvery.. The town was a nucleus centre of major political activity during the reign of the Cholas. The town was a hub of wealth, prosperity, trade and business activities. In this town lived an honest trader known as Amaranithi. He was a wealthy businessman and had plenty of rubies, diamonds, gold, and garments from all parts of the world. Still, his mind wondered only about 'pashupathi's 'feet. Amaranithi Nayanar served all devotees of the Lord, who wore snake rings. He gave them feasts enriched with his kind words and offered them loin clothes (Kovanam) to wear.

During the festival of the Three eyed Lord at Thirunallur, Nayanar constructed a shelter where devotees could take rest, have food and spend time thinking of God. One day the Lord decided to show that Amaranithi deserves fame to the entire world. He descended on earth and came to the abode of Nayanar in disguise with Shiva symbols and ash smeared all over His body.

On seeing him, the heart of Nayanar thrilled. He accorded a warm welcome to the bachelor. He asked the Lord, who had obscured His third eye, to stay in his abode and bless him. That Veda chanting bachelor replied that he would take a bath in the river Cauvery and come back.

Meanwhile, as it was about to rain, he entrusted his dried cloth (kovanam) to Nayanar and asked him to keep it safe.

Amaranithiyar kept it in a safe place with adequate security. When the bachelor returned, to his dismay Amaranithiyar found that the loin cloth had vanished from the box where he had kept it. He brought a new one instead, but the visitor refused to accept it. He wanted his own. "You call yourself a devotee of Shiva just to rob other devotees of their belongings" he shouted.

When Amaranithiyar sought to pacify him, he agreed to receive clothes equal in weight to the spare loincloth he was having. The shivering devotee fell at the bachelor's feet and offered gems and jewels to compensate for that cloth. He refused and said that He would accept only cloth that is equivalent of it. When asked how he could give the equivalent cloth, the devotees said whatever wet cloth He was wearing right then was the equivalent of the one he lost. So he asked Nayanar to give clothes equal to its weight.

Agreeing to His suggestion, Nayanar placed a balance instrument there. He put the wet cloth in one plate and on the other he kept on adding neatly woven clothes. Whatever, he placed; the plate with the cloth of the Bachelor weighed more. Surprised, he ordered to put all the new garment bags in the balance. That pile was not able to equate the magic cloth. Scared, he asked permission from the Lord to put his gems and other wealth too. He told that somehow He wanted things to be equivalent of His cloth. Amaranithiyar piled all his wealth.

Nothing happened. The true devotee who stood strong in serving the devotees, asked for permission to put himself, his wife and son to compensate. Feeling blessed, he with his son and wife circumambulated the balance where the Lord's cloth was there and said, "If it is true that the purity of love we did not fault in the God's Holy Ash's honest slavery, then it should come to balance." Chanting the Lord's name, he got on the plate over the piles of his wealth. The wholeness of love and dedication brought the balance of the instrument.

At that moment, the Lord with His Shakti appeared on the Holy Bull in the horizon. He blessed the devotee who with his family was standing on the plate. HE gave the wealth of being with Him. With the plate becoming the heavenly carrier, the devoted family reached the abode of Lord Shiva.

Somaeswar Temple, Pazhavara

- It is one of the 276 Padal Petra Shiva sthalams. It is also the 24th Shiva Stalam on the bank of river Cauveri in Chozha Nadu.
- Lore Shiva is Swayambumurthi (self manifested)
- The birth place of Amaranithi Nayanar, Mangayarkkarisiyar Nayanmar.
- There is no flag post in this temple

Amaranithi Nayanar of Pazhayari
Illustration courtesy: Ramalingar Pani Mandram

4

AANAYA NAYANAR

Thirumangalam is located near Trichy. The town is situated on the banks of a distributary of river Cauvery. Thirumangalam (near Lalgudi) was an important place of pilgrimage. The God who dwells in this village was called Samavedeeswarar. It was here that Samavedeeswarar purified Parasurama of the sin of killing his mother and also gave him the axe.

Aanaya was a handsome young shepherd who lived in this fertile village. He was tending cows and led his herds to rich pastures and clear pools. The animals grew healthy and strong. On his flute which he made, according to the laws of music, he would play the sacred five letters "Namashivaya". The villagers were thrilled by his divine music. He was a staunch devotee of Lord Shiva. He was devoted to Bhasma and also to Shiva Bakthas irrespective of their caste.

On a cloudy winter day, when he was playing the mantra on his instrument under the Konrai tree, the music captivated the cows and calves. The birds silently heard his music while the peacock danced to the tune. The animals sat silently and listened to his music. The river stopped its course. The music was so divine that it lured the celestials to earth to listen to his music. The divine music rose higher and higher and reached Heaven. Shiva and Parvathi also heard the music. The Panchakshara Mantra pleased them both. Both appeared before Nayanar and blessed him and took him to Kailas.

- Sri Samaveedeswrarar temple at Thirumangalam is 2000 years old and is considered equal in sacredness to Kasi and Gaya.
- Parasuraman, one of the ten avatars of Vishnu worshipped Shiva in this place to get rid of his Mathruhathi dosha. He got the dosha because of killing his mother. The place is also known as Parasurma Kshetram
- Chandikeswarar worshipped Shiva here to get rid of Pitruhathi dosha.
- Ravikuruva rishi was unhappy that there was no river here. Shiva made a river to flow here which is called "Gaya Panguni."

- Goddess Lakshmi worshipped Shiva here. Hence the place got the name Thirumangalam
- Saint Jaimini classified and interpreted Sama Veda in the precincts of the temple.
- The temple is believed to be a parihara sthalam incurred from neglecting ancestors.
- Sthala Vriksha is Jack Fruit tree.

5

APPUTHI ADIGAL NAYANAR

Adhinan marainul vaimai apputhiyarari nokki
Kathalar ivarkku mootha seiyunkattum munney
Meydhakku poothi chatha endralum vilaindha thanmai
Yathumon druraiyur ippothuingavan udhavan endrar......

Apputhi Adigal Nayanar lived in a village called Thingalur in the Chola kingdom. Thingalur is one of the famed 275 Thevaram Shiva sthalam. Here Lord Shiva is worshipped as Kailayanathar (Kailasanathar) with his consort Goddess Periyanayaki. It is in Thingalur that Chandran prayed to Lord Shiva and got his blessings. As Chandran is held in the locks of Lord Shiva, all devotees who worship Easwaran here, offer their prayers to this planet also.

The Devas and asuras were churning the ''paarkadal' using Mandira Malai and snake Vasuki. The asuras held the head portion of the snake and the devas, the tail portion. The poison emitted by Vasuki was consumed by Lord Shiva to save the devas, but the toxicity of venom affected the Devas who swooned on its impact. Along with the nectar (amirtham), Chandran emerged and it was he who revived the Devas.

Chandran is a very powerful god. He is credited as having the power to give life to all creatures. He is also revered as a god of fertility. Chandra has the ability to strengthen the mind, purify the blood and create positive energy and harmony among those who worship him. Chandra is said to be responsible for the dew that falls on plants at night and for the coming of nightfall. The cooling rays of the moon are very beneficial to all.

Thingalur is located 36kms from Kumbakonam, en route to Thiruvaiyaru. Chandran's wife is Rohini. The presiding deity is Kailasanathar and his consort Periyanayakiamman. Chandran is the Lord of Kadaga Rasi and he faces the East direction.

The mantra for moon is:

Aum Shrim krim cham chandeaye namah Aum.

Apputhi Adigal was from this holy place. He was an ardent follower of the great sage Thirunavukkarasar or Appar. Apputhi named his kids, cows, the cooking vessels, everything, in his house after the great saint. He established a lot of inns to feed devotees, dug ponds, and pitched many tents where cool water and drinks were served to weary travelers. All these also bore the name of Thirunavukkarasar.

During a visit to this town, Thirnivakkarasar was surprised to see his name everywhere. He came to know about the great devotion of Apputhi Adigal. Thirunavukkarasar arrived at Appudhi's home incognito. Apputhi welcomed him without knowing his real identity. Soon, Adigal came to know that he was Appar whom he had been worshipping, and was shocked and danced in ecstasy. Thirunavukkarasar consented to partake the meal offered in his honour. Appudi's wife prepared a grand feast. The couple asked their eldest son, Muthal Thirunavukkarasu to get the banana leaves to serve the food for the guest. When the boy cut the leaves, a snake bit him in the hand. The young boy rushed to hand over the leaves to his parents before the poison could kill him. He was determined not to reveal the snake bite as it would delay the feast to the devotee. The parents found out that the son died because of a snake bite. They covered their loving son in a mat and kept the body away from sight. Then, they rushed to the sage and served the feast. Thirunavukkarasar blessed the couple and their children with the holy ash. Then he asked about the eldest son as he wanted to bless him too. With something striking his heart Thirunavukkarasar asked Adikal to tell why his son was missing and what happened. Apputhi told him the truth. Then, Thirunavukkarasar carried the corpse to the temple of Lord Shiva in Thingalur. He sang ten songs in prayer to Lord Nilakanta (Shiva) who swallowed the poison 'Alahala' to save Devas to obliterate the power of poison infecting the innocent devotees. The hymns are called as 'Vidam TheerthaThiruppathikam'. All the devotees who sing these 10 holy hymns will be blessed by lord Shiva and even if a Snake bites them, will not die. Till today it is said that nobody has died in the vicinity of this temple due to snake bite. His prayer was answered and the boy came back to life. Thirnavukkarasar stayed for a few more days in Apputhi's house and sang a few verses about his devoted service.

Thingalur Temple

Kailasanathar

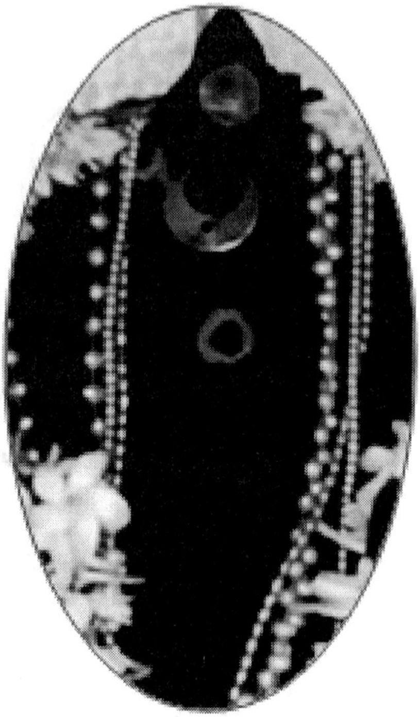

Sun God

6

ARUVALTAYA NAYANAR

In the Chola Kingdom, where river Ponni flows, was situated Kanamangalam, a fertile village. The village was located on the banks of the river Ponni. The village was picturesque with lovely lotus ponds and vast green paddy fields. The fields had plenty of golden crops. In the village lived a pious man called Tayanar, who spent his time offering rice, cabbage and tender mangoes to God.

He was a married man, working hard in the field. Even during extremely tough times, he toiled and received paddy as wages. He used to set apart the superior variety of paddy for God and the inferior ones for his family. Once, when the field yielded only superior paddy, Nayanar offered all of it to God. The family had only green leaves for consumption. Still they offered paddy, cabbage and tender mango to God.

A time came when even the greens got scarce, and the family had to live on water. Tayanar who was famished became very weak. Yet, he did not shrug his duties to God. One day while carrying his offering to God, he fell down due to starvation. The offerings fell on the ground and got muddy. Shattered, that he had to live even a day, without serving the Lord,Tayanar decided to end his life and pressed a small aruval (sword) to his throat.

God appeared and restrained the hand that held the sword. His wound on the throat miraculously healed within seconds. God accepted the dusty mangoes lying on the ground. Awed and overwhelmed with joy, he sang in praise of Shiva and declared himself as his eternal slave. Lord Shiva then appeared with Parvathi atop the holy bull and blessed him, saying that he had attained salvation. Tayanar was christened as "Aruval Taya" Nayanar

Aruvaltaya Nayanar temple

Aruvaltaya Nayanar
Illustration courtesy: Ramalingar Paini Mandram

7

CHANDESA NAYANAR

Chandesa Nayanar is one of the five forms that are worshipped in all the temple festivals even today. Others are Vinayagar, Subramanyar, Somaskandar and Sakthi. He has a special place in all the temples, where the water after anointing the Lord falls out. Devotees leaving the temple after worship must take the permission from Chandesa.

Chandesa Nayanar was born in the town called Seigalur along the banks of river Manni. Under Chola rule, the town flourished naturally and intellectually. The town was occupied by great Vedic scholars and the people were pious and God fearing. The great scholars passed on the knowledge of Vedas and agamas to the younger generation. Among the people who chanted Vedas in the town lived a person called Yaksha Dattan in the Kashyapa Gothram. He and his wife was a devoted couple, much given to charity and service. He was also compassionate to human beings and animals, in which he saw the Divine. Vicharasarma was born to Yaksha Dattan. When Vicharasarma was seven, his parents performed upanayanam for him.

The young lad possessed the capacity to learn the Vedas and rituals faster to the astonishment of the villagers.

One day, Vicharasarma saw a cowherd savagely beating a pregnant cow with a rod. He couldn't bear to see the sight. He explained the nobility of the animal, its usefulness and how it consumes hay and fodder that we have no use for, but delivers milk and dung, both useful to us. He told the cowherd that he would take over the control of the cows. He took the cows every morning to places where they got plenty of grass. If there was not enough grass, he would pluck and give it to them. He cleaned them well, scrubbing and scratching them, while they had their fill of water in the pond. After they got enough food and water he would make them rest in a cool shady place and played on his flute while they chewed cud. He also protected them from the attack of other animals. The cows loved him dearly for the tender care and automatically yielded abundant milk whenever he touched them. He also gave the milk to the owner of the cow without interruption. The people of the town were very happy.

As he took care of the cows, he also attended to his spiritual pursuits. He took a bath in the river and collected peepul twigs for the holy pyre and chanted "Aum" as he returned home. Being a Shiva devotee, he could sense the positive vibrations under an ebony tree on the sand hills along the riverside. He made a Lingam there and ceremoniously performed bath (abhishekam) with milk. The cows happily gave more milk and participated in his prayers by their close presence.

One day a passerby witnessed the scene and carried the story to the cowherd, who promptly conveyed the matter to Yaksha Dattan. He told Yaksha that his son's indulgence in performing abhishekam has cost him huge monetary loss. Yaksha Dattan promised proper action to prevent any such thing happening in the future. He came back home after the evening worship. He didn't tell anything to his son, but wanted to find out for himself what happened. After Nayanar started from home with the cows, he followed him stealthily and hid behind a tree to see what his son was doing.

Vicharasarma made a Lingam and bathed it with milk. Then, he decorated it with beautiful flowers and sat in meditation. The father got angry and beat him with a stick and ordered him to stop the divine routine. Unperturbed, Sarma continued his offerings. Yaksha Dattan got furious and kicked the pot of milk. Sarma considering this as interference took a stick that was nearby. It became an axe. He threw it on Yaksha which cut his legs and he fell down on the sand. The devotee continued with his worship.

It was then that the divine light of Uma Parameswara engulfed him. A mystic voice declared that Vicharasarma would henceforth be their Chandes, since he injured even his father for the sake of Shiva. Chandesa was proclaimed as the son of the divine couple. He was allowed all the freedom to wear what the Lord wore and eat what he ate. Shiva made him the head of his devotees and said "Everything, the vessels of food, the ornaments and dress offered are for you after my usage" and you are given the name "Chandishan" (Chandikesvarar) and crowned his hair with konrai garland with the crescent in it. His father's leg was healed and the family was escorted to Shivaloka.

The devotion of Chandishan has many references in the twelve Thirumurais.

Photo courtesy: Ethirajan Srinivasan

Lord Shiva crowning Chandeesa Nayanar with his laburnum garland: Gangai Konda Choza puram temple,

Courtsy: Ramilngar Pani Mandram

8

CHERAMAN PERUMAL NAYANAR

Cheraman Perumal Nayanar was born in Kodunkolur. It was the capital city of Malai Nadu. He was born in the royal family of Kothayars, known as the Uthiyan family. The name Cheraman was the common name for all Cheras. Perumal was the title adopted by him after his coronation. His original name was Perumakkodai. He had great devotion to the Lord, even as a child. When he came of age, he renounced the world and went to Tiruvanchaikulam and engaged himself in the worship of the Lord there.

The country was ruled by Sengolporayan, who also renounced the world. He had no issues and the throne was vacant. They went to Tiruvanchaikalam and requested Perumakkodai to ascend the throne. He bowed to the divine will. He went to the temple and offered a prayer. The Lord permitted him to accept the ruler ship. He ruled the country justly and wisely. He could understand all languages, even the language of the birds. The Lord bestowed on him all the aiswaryas, strength, royal vehicles, etc.

After the coronation, he went to the temple and after worshipping the Lord, was returning to the palace. On the way, he saw a washerman whose body had been smeared with white sand and mud. The very sight enraptured Cheraman who saw in him the image of Lord Shiva with the sacred ash smeared all over the body. He was raised to God-consciousness. He descended from the elephant and fell at the feet of the washerman, in spite of the latter's protest.

By his many acts of devotion and piety, he earned the grace of Lord Shiva. The Lord sent to him a renowned musician and devotee, Banapatirar, with a palm leaf on which was the Lord's own song in praise of Cheraman! It read: 'Oh king who honours great poets with rich presents, who rules his subjects with love! Glory to you! I am very highly pleased with your devotion and charitable nature". The bearer of this message is Banapatirar who is a great devotee like you. He is a great musician and always sings my glories on his favourite instrument, Yazh. He has come to see you. Welcome him with due respects and honour him with plenty of riches.'

Cheraman welcomed the musician with great love and devotion. When he read the song of the Lord, he was overjoyed and rolled on the ground. He said to Banapatirar: 'Oh noble soul, kindly take possession of all these and accept my kingdom also.' Banapatirar was astounded to witness the king's devotion and said: 'Oh king, I am highly pleased with your Darshan. I shall accept only what is absolutely necessary for me, for that has been the command of the Lord.' He took what he needed and left Kodunkolur on an elephant. Cheraman escorted him up to the border.

Cheraman was greatly devoted to Lord Nataraja. He would worship the Lord daily, and, by His grace, at the time of prayer, would hear the musical sound produced by the Lord's anklets during His dance. One day, at the time of the prayer, he did not hear the usual divine sound. Cheraman was greatly afflicted at heart. He thought that he must be guilty of a great crime and decided to end his life. At once he heard the divine sound and a voice in the sky explained: 'Oh noble soul, my friend (Sundarar) Nambi Arurar has come to Tillai and was singing sweet Tamil songs. I was completely absorbed in that and hence the delay in blessing you with the musical sound of my anklet.' The Lord wanted to create a friendship between Sundarar and Cheraman and so spoke highly of Sundarar to Cheraman.

Cheraman, desirous of meeting Sundarar, at once started for Tillai. The very sight of the Lord in Tillai entranced him. He sang 'Pon Vannathu Anthadi' on Lord Nataraja. In appreciation, the Lord blessed him with the musical sound of His anklets. Before Cheraman reached Tillai, Sundarar had already left the place. Cheraman therefore proceeded to Tiruvarur where he met Sundarar. They embraced each other and fell at each other's feet. They became fast friends. At Tiruvarur, Cheraman composed the famous 'Tiru Mummanikovai' on Lord Thiagaraja.

Then they went to Vedaranyam. There Cheraman sang his 'Tiruanthati' on the Lord. After visiting many shrines on the way they came to Madura. The Pandyan king welcomed them. The Chola prince who was staying with the Pandyan king also welcomed them. In their company the great saints visited many shrines. Taking leave of the kings, Cheraman and Sundarar returned to Tiruvarur. From there, at the request of Cheraman, Sundarar accompanied him to Kodunkolur. There Cheraman took Sundarar on an elephant and went round the city.

When Sundarar returned to Tiruvarur, he instructed Cheraman to rule the country justly and wisely.

Cheraman obeyed the saint's commands. On the next occasion Sundarar visited Kodunkolur, he suddenly left the place and went to the sacred shrine at Tiruvanchaikalam where he sought the Lord's grace and attained Liberation. By intuition, Cheraman learnt of Sundarar's release and he also attained the Lotus Feet of the Lord.

Thiruvanchikulam Mahadeva Temple

9

DANDI ADIGAL NAYANAR

Dandi Adigal Nayanar was born in Thiruvarur in the Chola Kingdom. He was born blind. He was a great devotee of Shiva. He often used to visit the Shiva Temple at Thiruvarur. At that time, many Jain temples encroached upon the premises of Shiva temple, Thiuvarur. The town was a prominent Jain settlement.

Dandi Adigal was also a prominent Shiva devotee. Seeing the encroachment of temple land he decided to rebuild the temple tank whose western bank was occupied by Jain houses. The blind Adigal erected a post where the earth is needed to be dug and tied a rope to it. He erected another post and tied the rope. He stared digging the land with a spade and collected the mud in a basket. Then he walked back to the bank holding the rope for safety and emptied the basket. The Jains who were very conventional felt that digging of earth will kill many micro –organisms and insects. Harming or killing even a small insect is considered as a great in Jainism. They ridiculed the efforts of Adigalar and removed the posts. They also snatched the spade and the basket. Jain also said that they will leave the town if Lord Shiva restored his eyesight. Adigalar appealed to Shiva for help.

Shiva appeared in the Dandi Adigal's dream and promised to help. Shiva the appeared in the Chola King's dream and asked him to resolve the problem faced by his devotee.

Adigal's eye sight was restored. Jains, who were hurt and prevented Adigal from his duty, became blind. The King ordered the renovation of the tank temple and completed it quickly.

Thiruvarur Thiyagaraja Temple

Panchandeeswarar Temple Thruvarur.

Thiruvarur Thiyagarajar Ther

Dandi Adigal Nayanar
Illustration courtesy: Ramalingar Paini Mandram

10

ENADINATHA NAYANAR

The sacred ash has a mystic power,
'Tis worn by the dwellers in the sky.
The ash bestows true loveliness.
Praise of the ash ascends on high.
The ash shows what the tantras mean
And true religion's essence tells,
The ash of Him the Alavay,
In whom red –lipped Uma dwells

–Sambandar

Enadinatha Nayanar was a Shanar (toddy tapper). He was born in Eyinanur in Chola Kingdom. It is situated to the south-east of Kumbakonam on the banks of the river Arisol. It was very fertile and rich.

Enadinathar was an ardent devotee of Lord Shiva. To Enadiar, the three white lines of Vibhuti or sacred ash on one's forehead were sufficient to evoke his reverence.

The sacred marks of holy ashes are capable of removing all the impurities like desires, worldly bondages, illusion etc in one's life and provide ultimate wisdom about the eternal truth. The Shastras assure us that the sacred ash is a divine healer. It cures all diseases, including the disease of birth and death, and bestows on the devotee who wears it, the highest wealth, viz., Moksha.

No wonder Enadiar worshipped whoever came to him with the ash on his forehead. Enadiar saw the Lord Shiva in him. He was even ready to lay down his life at the feet of the devotee who wore the ash.

Enadinatha Nayanar was a very good swordsman. He was a tutor to the princes in fencing. He earned a good income from his profession. He spent his income in the service of the Shiva Bhaktas. This evoked the jealousy of another man belonging to the same profession. His name was Atisuran (a great hero). He was not strong or skilled in the martial arts. He was full of vices. Yet, he wanted to fight Enadinathar and defeat him.

One day Atisuran marched towards Enadinathar's house, with all his relatives, fully armed. He hoped to defeat Enadinathar, with the help of his relatives. He stood in front of Enadinathar's house and challenged him to a fight. Enadinathar accepted the challenge and came forward. Atisuran got frightened. He asked Enadinathar to come to the nearby grove to fight with him. The relatives of Atisuran were waiting in the grove. In the meantime, friends of Enadinathar had also gathered around him. The two parties fell on each other, and in the terrible fight, many lives were lost. Atisuran ran away from the grove. He wanted to kill Enadinathar, not in open fight but by stratagem.

The next day, he sent a message to Enadinathar: 'Let us fight again, but without any assistance this time: otherwise, many innocent people die on our account. Let us go to a lonely place, without anyone's knowledge and fight.' Enadinathar accepted it. The next morning, Enadinathar went away secretly and was awaiting Atisuran's arrival at the stipulated place. Atisuran, with the sacred ashes on his forehead approached Enadinathar. Enadinathar pounced upon him. In a moment, Atisuran removed the shield, revealing the sacred ashes. Enadinathar quickly lowered his sword and thought: 'what a sin I was about to commit! He has become a Shiva Bhakta now. I must not harm him. Let him achieve his object of killing me.' Endinathar wanted to throw the sword away, but kept it in his hand, else he would be compelling his opponent to incur the sin of killing an unarmed person. As he was mutely standing thus, Atisuran killed him. Lord Shiva was highly pleased with this self-sacrificing devotion that Enadinathar had for the ashes. HE appeared before Enadinathar, and took him to His Abode. The Tamil month of Purattasi, Uthradam, is widely celebrated as Guru Puja Day to commemorate this incident.

Brahmapureeswarar Temple, Enanallur

11

ERIPATHA NAYANAR

Pasupatheendu patheem dharanipatheem,
Bhujaloka patheem cha sathipatheem,
Pranatha bhaktha janarthi haram param,
Bhajatha re manuja girijapatheem.

Pray to the lord of the daughter of the mountain,
Who is the lord of all beings,
Who is the lord of the moon,
Who is the lord of the world,
Who is the lord of the universe,
Who is the Lord of Sathi Devi,
And who destroys the sorrows of his devotees.
(Pasupathi Ashtakam. Trans by P R Ramachandar)

Karuvur was one of the important capitals of the Chola kings. It was a beautiful town with natural scenic green surroundings adding serenity, divinity and filled with devotees of Shiva. The town had an ancient Anili temple of Lord Pashupathi Iswar and the river Ambiravati flowing along the town, provided a nice and cool atmosphere for the saints and sages to sit on its banks and perform tapas.

The chants and the prayers mingled with the breeze and spread a positive spiritual vibration across the tiny town. The people of the green village were ever green with the blessings of Pashupathi Iswar and enjoyed only happiness. The town had a devotee named Eripath Nayanar whose only mission and ambition was to please and serve Shiva Bhaktas or devotees. He always carried an axe with him to protect the Shiva devotees and used it if anyone tried to to be violent or harm them.

In the same place lived another Shiva Bhakta named Sivakami Andar. He was an ardent devotee of Shiva and regularly worshipped Lord Shiva. At dawn, he would take a dip in the river and walk around the lush garden to pick colourful flowers. He would then meticulously make nice looking garlands to take to the temple to offer to the God. He religiously followed this daily routine without fail. He would always rush to the temple to offer the garland on time for Puja.

On a Maha Navami day when the devotees and the people were joyous, Sivakami Andar was rushing to the temple with equal happiness and devotion with a basket of flower and garland. As Sivakami Andar was hurrying, the King's pet elephant was coming back from the river after its bath. On the elephants back were two Mahouts and three assistants were escorting the elephant. All of a sudden, the elephant became mad and caught hold of Andavar, snatched the basket of flowers, threw it on the ground and ran away. The flowers were scattered on the ground. Infuriated by the action of the elephant and feeling guilty for not reaching the flowers to God, he chased the elephant in a fit of rage. Old age prevented him from running fast. Exhausted, he fell down and wept bitterly, saying "Shivada, Shivada" in agony. At that time Eripatha Nayanar happened to pass that way. He heard Sivakami Andar's story about the elephant. He asked Andar the direction in which the elephant had galloped and he ran fast to catch the elephant. Soon he overtook the elephant and hurled his axe which hit the elephant and it died instantly. He did not spare the Mahouts and killed them too.

The news of the incident spread like wild fire and reached the King's ears. The King rushed on his horse to the spot where his pet elephant was killed. The king also had an army of soldiers accompanying him. The king could not see who had killed the elephant. He was not able to associate the death of the elephant with Shiva Yogi Eripathar. While the king was in a great dilemma and puzzled, a passerby pointed his finger at the Shiva Yogi making it clear that he had killed the elephant. Instead of getting angry, the King wanted to know what prompted the Yogi to kill the elephant. He imagined that he must have done so to defend himself from the attack of the elephant. The King jumped from the horse's back and asked the devotee what was the crime the elephant and guards had committed to get such a severe punishment.

Eripathar told him that the elephant in its madness had committed a great misdeed against the service of God. The King fell at the feet of Eripathar and said that he also deserved a death punishment as his elephant was responsible for hindering the flower reaching God. He requested Eripathar to kill him also as a sentence. The king pleaded with the devotee to kill him with his sword and not with the axe. The belief of the king and his reverence towards Lord's devotees moved Nayanar. Eripathar, instead of killing the king, raised the sword and cut off his own head. Everyone was shocked including the king. Tears poured down the king's eyes. The crowd wept.

At the very moment, God said: Oh! People of exceeding love and devotion for me, I have just shown the greatness of my devotee and the king's consciousness to be in the path of virtue. Suddenly, the elephant, the guard and Eripathar, flowers and garlands found their way magically to Sivakami Andar.The proud and pious king took Eripathar in a procession holding a royal umbrella over his head. Both went to the temple and offered prayers to Pashupathi Iswar. Eripathar continued to be in the service of the Lord and soon became the head of Shivaganangal on reaching Kailasam.

Sri Kalayana Pasupatheeswarar Temple, Karur

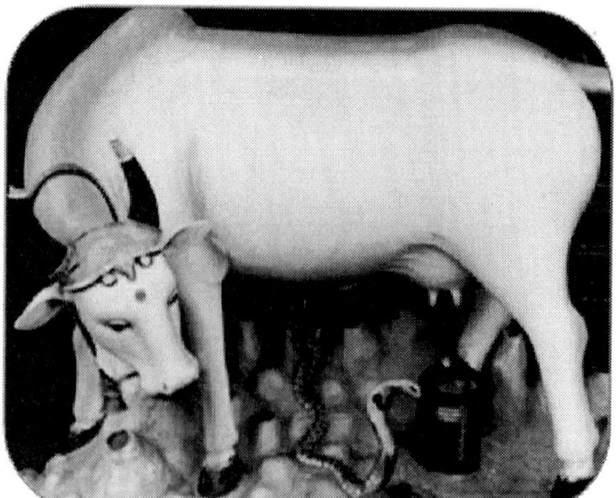

Eripatha Nayanar
Illustration courtesy: Ramalingar Paini Mandram

12

EYARKON KALIKAMA NAYANAR

Eyarkon Kalikama Nayanar lived in Thirumangalam, Ponni Nadu. He belonged to the family called "Eyarkudi" which produced Commander-in-Chief for the Chola kings. Kalikama Nayanar was a devoted devotee of Lord Shiva. Kalikama Nayanar was a contemporary of Sundaramurthy Nayanar. Once he heard the news that Lord has sent Sundarar to settle a domestic dispute.

Kalikama Nayanar was unable to digest this action of the Lord and got infuriated. Sundarar came to know about Nayanar's reaction and appealed to god to appease Kalaikamar's anger. Lord Shiva immediately made Kalikamar suffer from severe colic and appeared in his dream and said that only Sundarar can cure him. Kalikamar preferred to end his life rather than be treated by Sundarar. He gave up his life by cutting his bowel open. Sundarar was not allowed to see Kalikamar's body. In desperation, Sundarar attempted to cut his throat to end his life. At that moment, Lord Shiva appeared and stopped Sundarar's suicidal bid. He also gave life to Kalikamar. Both Sundarar and kalikamar embraced each other in joy.Kalikamar spent the rest of his life in the service of the Lord and finally reached Shiva's abode.

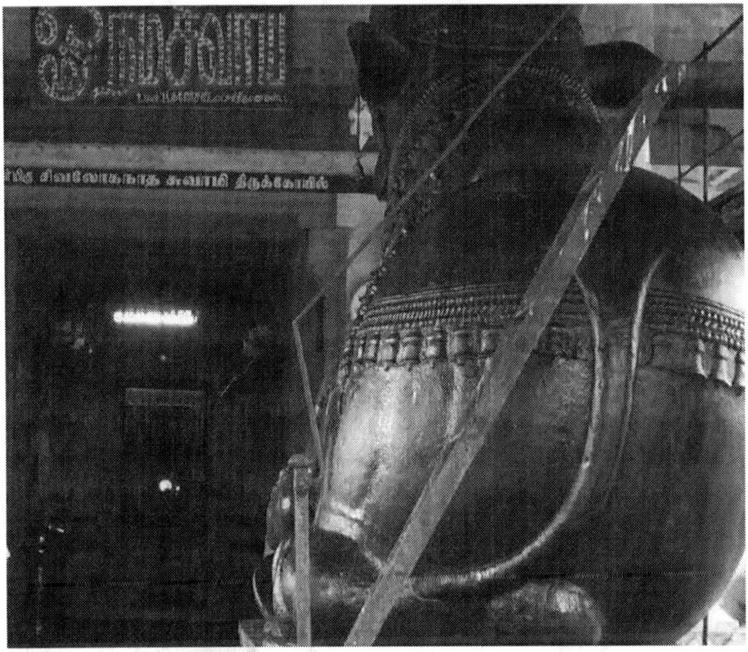

Pancha Lingam: Thirupunganur

13

GANANATHA NAYANAR

Gananatha Nayanar is the 37th Nayanar. Gananatha means the head of the group of Ganas or attendants of Shiva who live in Kailas. This pious Shiva devotee was born in a Brahmin family in Sirkazhi in Chola kingdom.

Sirkazhi is situated between Mayiladuthurai and Chidambaram. It is a typical south Indian small town with a serene atmosphere all around. The people of Sirkazhi have still preserved their traditional customs and rituals. There are many mythological stories associated with Sirkazhi.

According to one such story, this is the place where Lord Shiva appeared when the entire world was submerged under water. The Sirkazhi temple has about 20 Thirthas in its complex. Brahma Tirtha is the most important of them. According to mythology it is the place where Lord Brahma offered his prayer to Lord Shiva. It is also believed that by taking a dip in this Thirtha one gets rid of his or her sins.

Gananatha Nayanar used to worship the Lord of Sirkazhi, Tiru Thoniappar, and the Lord who serves as a boat to cross the ocean of samsara. Nayanar occupied himself in various temple activities to please the Lord. In the early mornings, after a bath and chanting of Panchakshara, he used to go to the garden to pluck the fragrant flowers for worship. He enjoyed rendering all kinds of services and also discussed with the people, about the glory of Tonniappar.He used to make nice garlands and give them to the temple. He would then draw pure water from the tanks and wells and supply to the temple. He would then sweep the temple precincts. He would clean all the lamps, place new wicks and oil for burning. He also had a practice of copying the verses from the scriptures and giving it to others for singing and he himself would sing them. All these services, alone made him a slave of Shiva and he merged with Shiva in a ripe age. In the month of Panguni, Thiruvathirai is celebrated as Guru Puja Day, the day Gananatha Nayanar attained the abode of Lord Shiva.

Sirkazhi – Bhramapureeswarar Temple

14

IDANGAZHI NAYANAR

I am servitor of glorious Idangkazhi, the great one
That wears a garland of petalled flowers
Thiru Thonda Thogai

Idankaliyar was a saint, venerated in Saivisam. He was an Irukku Velir chieftain, who is described to not only have pardoned a devotee of Lord Shiva, who stole from the royal granaries, but also distributed rice to devotees of Shiva.

Idangazhi was born and lived in Kodumpalur, Tamil Nadu. He was one of the Irukku Velir petty chieftains who served the Chola kings. He is said to have descended from the Yadavas of Dwarka who migrated to South with sage Agastya. He is also described to be part of theKalabha interregnum, a period between 3rd and 7th century.

Idangazhi was the chieftain of the kingdom of Konadu, whose capital was Kodumbalur. He was a staunch devotee of Shiva. He lived and governed by Shaivite ways and made arrangements for worship of Shiva in temples as per the Agama scriptures. There was also another devotee of Shiva in Konadu. He had taken the vow of serving and feeding Shiva's devotees. He suddenly became poor and could not get food to feed a devotee of Shiva. To complete his vow, he entered the royal granaries to steal rice, but was caught red-handed by the guards. The arrested devotee was presented to Idangazhi, who understood the rationale of the intended burglary. He pardoned the devotee and let him free. He realized the futility of a full go-down when devotees of Shiva were going hungry. Idangazhi made announcements throughout the kingdom that devotees of Shiva can come and take away not only rice from the granary, but also other riches from the treasury, as much as they wanted. Idangazhi was instrumental in the spread of Shaivism and thus gained the grace of Shiva. In Periya Puranam Idamghzhi is described as the ancestor of the Chola king Aditya (871-907CE).Idangazhi Nayanar is specially worshipped in the month of Aippasi.

Moovar Koil, Kodumbalur

Photo Courtesy: Ramesh.M. *Moovar Koil, Kodumbalur*

Idangazhi Nayanar: Illustration courtesy: Ramalingar Paini Mandram

15

ILAIYANKUDI MARA NAYANAR

Ilayankudi Mara Nayanar was a farmer and ardent devotee of Lord Shiva. He lived in a tiny village called Ilayankudi. He was a true vellala, straight forward and hardworking. Mara Nayanar owned plenty of lands and was a keen farmer and had divine blessing. He believed that God appeared in the form of human beings, and he was generous and kind to all the devotees who served God. His dutiful wife was an embodiment of all virtues. They both strove to serve their guests who are Shiva devotees. Mara Nayanar practiced the sadhna known as Mahewsara Puja which is the worship of the devotees of Maheswara or Shiva.

It is described as follows:

'On seeing a devotee of Lord Shiva, with the external marks of Vibhuti, Rudraksham, etc., taking him as Lord Shiva Himself, welcoming him, prostrating before him, washing his hands and feet, drinking that water (Charanamrit), giving him a seat, worshipping him with flowers, Doopa, Deepa, and Naivedya, pleasing him with sweet words, thanking the Lord for the opportunity, and accompanying the guest for some distance while sending him away—these constitute Maaheswara Puja. This is also included in Chariyai (Source: Divine life).

Offering food to the Lord's devotees had purified his heart and made him a fit receptacle for the grace of God. Nayanar had been blessed with all the wealth of the world. But, he considered that the wealth belonged to the Lord, to be utilised for the benefit of His devotees.

Lord Shiva was pleased with the Nayanar's devotion. He wanted to show to the world that His devotee would be undaunted by the worst calamity and would remain unshaken in his virtue. Nayanar's wealth melted away. His wealth had left him, but not his virtue. On the contrary, his devotion to the Lord and His devotees grew more and more intense. Nayanar sold all his property and had to sell even himself in order to be able to serve the devotees of the Lord.

One day it was raining heavily. Nayanar and his wife were starving. No one came forward to help them. Finally, he bolted the door and was about to fall asleep. Just then he heard a knock at the door, and, on opening it, found a Shiva Bhakta standing in front of the house, drenched in rain. Nayanar at once took the guest inside, dried his body and gave him fresh clothes to wear. 'Rest awhile, Swami, while we prepare some food for you to appease your hunger,' said Nayanar and told his wife of his predicament: there was nothing to offer the devotee of the Lord. But, the devout wife suggested that Nayanar could go into the backyard and collect the grain-seeds that they had just sown that very day. Nayanar accepted the suggestion. On account of the heavy rain, the grains were floating and it was easy to collect them in a basket. As soon as he brought the grains, the wife fried and crushed them, and with the help of some greens that grew in their own backyard, cooked a nice dinner for the guest.

Nayanar was supremely happy. And, as he went to awaken the guest, he discovered that he had disappeared. At the same time, Nayanar saw in sky, Lord Shiva Who had come in the form of the devotee and Mother Parvathy showering their blessing on him and his wife. The Lord said: 'Oh noble souls, I am highly pleased with your devotion. You will soon attain My Abode and live there forever.'

Yaelavar kuzhalal thnoodu
Eda vahanai thonri
Katchi thnthu odkontar

Shiva blessed the couple saying that such devotees without the least attachment to wealth are the ideal person to protect all the wealth. Hence, the right place for you is heaven. Please come.

Sundarar, who was astounded by the devotion and detachment of Ilayankudi Nayanar, sang in praise of him saying that he is the best devotee of Shiva.

Illayankudi Mara Nayanar bringing the seeds sown in the field for feeding the monk.

16

ISAIGNANIYAR

Isaignaniyar was born in the Brahmin caste during 12 century AD.She was pious and an ardent devotee of Lord Shiva. She lived in the holy village of Tirunavalur. Her son, the great Saiva hagiologist was born here. Her husband Sadaiya Nayanar was also a Nayanmar.She is considered as the last in the list of 63 Nayanmars. Due to her devotion to Shiva and also because she is the mother of Sundarar, she got recognition as a Nayanar.

Tirunavalur

This is the 8th of the 22 Tevara Stalms in Tamil Nadu. During the churning of the ocean, one drop of nectar fell here, and grew into a Naval Tree. After few centuries, this temple was built. The place was named as Navalur and deity was called Navaleeswarar.

17

IYARPAGAI NAYANAR

Iyarpagai Nayanar of Cauveri-Poompattinam, was a very generous man and offered alms in plenty, to the Shiva yogis. Lord Shiva wanted the entire world to know about this benevolent nature of Iyarpagai and decided to put him to a test.

One day, He came to Iyarpagai's house in the disguise of a Shaiva Brahmin. He requested Iyarpagai to give him his wife so that she could stay with him and serve him. Iyarpagai agreed without any hesitation and his wife too did not utter a single word. The three of them left for the Yogi's home.

The village people were enraged when they came to know about this. Iyarpagai, who had accompanied them as a bodyguard, attacked all the people including his own kith and kin who objected to this. When they almost reached the Brahmin's town, Iyarpagai bowed to the Brahmin with respect and left without turning back even once.

Suddenly he heard the Brahmin calling out his name. When he rushed back, the Brahmin was not to be seen anywhere. He had disappeared and only his own wife was to be seen. In the next instant, Lord Shiva and Goddess Parvathi appeared before the couple and blessed him.

Cauveripoompattinam poompuhar

Old port city in Cauveripattinam/
Source: www.nio.org

18

KALIKAMBA NAYANAR

Kalikamba Nayanar is one of the 63 saints listed in the Periya Puranam. He was born in Pennagadam in the Cauvery delta region, near Cuddalore, during the time of Chola King Kochengan, in the Sangam era. Kalikama was a Vaisya by caste. He was totally dedicated to the devotees of Shiva in whom he saw the God himself. Kalikama considered it his duty, to sell goods at a reasonable price to all. He spent his wealth in feeding and taking care of Shiva devotees. He was visiting Sri Pralayakaleswarar temple daily, after his bath.

The temple is praised in the hymns of Saint Tirunavukarasar. It is in this temple that the saint appealed to Lord Sudarakozhundhu Nathar to inscribe on him, the symbols of the trident and his Nandi- Vrushba. Lord honoured the saint.

The reputation of this temple is beyond imagination. Indira, the king of Devas needed flowers from Earth to perform Shiva Puja in his place. He sent two maidens to earth to bring flowers. They found flowers here were beautiful and stayed back. On seeing a Shiva lingam in the garden, they began doing pujas. As they did not return, Indira sent the Divine cow Kamadenu to bring them back. Kamadenu found the maidens and he too joined them in the Shiva puja by pouring its milk on the Lord. As she too did not return, Indira sent his white elephant Iravadham in search of them. The elephant, seeing them in worship, joined the camp and stood such a way creating a cool shadow so that Sun did not hurt the Shivalinga. Finally, Indira himself came down, saw the maids, cow and the elephant and also joined them in the worship. All returned together with the blessings of Lord Shiva. This is the birthplace of celebrated saints Kalikamba Nayanar, Meikandar and Saint Maraignana Sambandar of the Saivite Guru tradition.

Kalikama Nayanar who lived here always welcomed the large number of Shiva devotees to his home and fed them well. One day, a devotee came to this town. He was invited to Nayanar's house. Kalikama asked his wife to fetch water to wash the devotee's feet before dinner. She brought the water in a big vessel. Kalikama asked his wife to take a mug full of water and pour it on the devotee's feet to enable him to wash his feet. Kalikama's wife picked up the mug with water and looked at the devotees face. She recognized him as a lowly servant who served in her house a few years back. She was reluctant to pour water. Kalikama became angry, took a sword and severed her hands. She fell down wreathing in great pain and bleeding. Kalikama poured the water and was about to wash the devotee's feet. Suddenly the devotee disappeared. There was sudden effulgence from earth to heaven and Kalikama merged with the effulgence.

The saint proved the truth which Sage Narada emphasized in his work 'Bhakti Sutras': there is no distinction of caste, creed or status, among the devotees of the Lord.

Sri Pralayakaleswarar temple

- This is one of the 276 Devara Padal Petra Shiva Stalams.
- This is the birth place of Kalikamba Nayanar and Meikandar-the first of the four "Santhan Kuravars." He is considered a pioneer of Saiva philosophy. Ganasambandar also believed to have lived here

19

KALIA NAYANAR

Kalia Nayanar was an oil monger of Thiruvotriyur. He was an ardent devotee of Lord. Shiva. He took upon himself the duty of lighting the temple lamps daily. To test his devotion, the Lord made him very poor. Kalia Nayanar was handicapped as he could not have resources to buy oil. His relatives turned him down when he approached them for help. He began to work as a laborer to earn money for the oil. This effort did not last long. He became poorer and failed to continue his duty. In despair he decided to cut his throat and use the blood instead of oil to light the temple lamps. He began cutting his throat when the Lord appeared in front of him with his consort on the holy bull amidst Vedic chanting and blessed Kalia Nayanar for his devotion. Kalia Nayanar lived happily for many years and attained the abode of the Lord.

Thiruvotriyur temple and Goddess

This is the venue where Saint Sundarar married Sangiliyar under the Magizham tree. Saint Pattinathar attained liberation here. The temple was also visited by Sant Arunagirinathar and Ramalinga Vallalar.Saint Tyagaraja visited the temple and composed five songs on Goddess

Thyagaraja Temple

20

KANAMPULLA NAYANAR

Kanampulla Nayanar was a grass cutter, selling the Kanampul grass used for wicks in Shiva temples. He was born in a farming family in a tiny village called Irrukivelur in Sirkazi Taluk. Kanampulla Nayanar spent all his money lighting lamps in various Shiva temples. The Nayanar sang hymns to Shiva and devotedly served Shiva and his devotees. The Lord in Irukkivelur is believed to cure the bonds of births apart from the various diseases, the body accumulates. Irukkivelur is now called "Pelur" (Salem District). With its huge temple and tall tower, it beckons seekers from all over to relax under the Holy feet of the Lord with his consort, Aramvalarthanayaki.

Kanampulla Nayanar's wealth quickly vanished. He then moved to Thillai Nataraja Temple, Chidambaram and felt a new strength in his soul. He earned his living by cutting grass and selling kanampul grass. With the money he earned, he purchased ghee and began to light lamps in nearby temples of Tirupuliavaram. This is the holy place where Vyagrapada lived, in inner communion with Nataraja, the dancing form of Shiva.

One day he could not sell the straws he brought in spite of his best efforts. He had nothing else in his hand.

Unperturbed, he went ahead burning the straws to illuminate the temple. As the stacks of impurities gets burnt quickly, when the devotion for Lord Shankara enters, all the straws he had, were over and he required more to illuminate the temple. Unwilling to stop the service, Kanampulla Nayanar pulled out the hair from his head and used it in place of the straw. Shiva appreciating the flawless love appeared before him and released him from the cycle of rebirths.

The Vaitheeswaran temple dedicated to him is located in Pullirukkuveloor. The Tamil month of karthikai - Kiruthikai star is widely celebrated as Guru Puja Day of Kanampulla Nayanar.

21

KANNAPPA NAYANAR

There was a family of hunters, headed by Nagan, who lived in a village called Uduppur.The village belonged to the kingdom of Pothappinadu, a beautiful lush green land in natural surroundings. Nagan,the chief hunter and his wife Thathai had no child. Both Nagan and his wife were very skilled in the art of archery. They hunted animals with their folks for livelihood. Nagan and his wife were ardent devotees of Lord Muruga. They prayed to Muruga to give them a child. Thathai soon gave birth to a child. The child was dark complexioned and strong. They affectionately called him "Thinnan".

His parents decided to teach him archery and the day of his first lesson was a great occasion for the villagers. There was a great celebration. Soon Thinnan became a proficient archer. Thinnan's father grew old and found it difficult to carry out his job as the chief hunter. Thinnan was made the new chief of their clan.

One day, Thinnan went on his hunting trip. While chasing a big pig, Thinnan and his two companions Nadan and Kadan lost their way. They continued chasing the pig and arrived at the foothills of Thiru Kalahasthi. The three of them were too tired, hungry and thirsty. Thinnan finally killed the pig, which they had chased for a long time. He assigned the job of cooking the meat to Kadan.

Thinnan left with Nadan to fetch some water from the river. He was amazed at the sight of the hill and a huge temple on the hilltop. He decided to climb the hill after hearing from Nadan about the temple of Kudumithevar (Lord with a tuft). Nadan followed Thinnan. At the top of the hill, they saw a big Lingam. Emotionally moved, Thinnan hugged and kissed the Lingam. He continued to stay in the same position and felt relieved from a heavy weight from his shoulders. He decided to stay there and safeguard the Lord. His thoughts were dominated by affection towards the Lord. Nadan taught Thinnan the method of worship of the Lord.

Thinnan wanted to offer food, feeling that the Lord might be hungry, and flowers to decorate Him. He walked down the hill to fetch a mouthful of water and showered it on the Lingam. He decorated the Lingam with the flowers which he had on his head. He served the Lord with the best part of the meat after tasting it. After finishing his performance of Abishekam, Alangaram and Naivedyam to the Lord, Thinnan sat at the entrance to safeguard the Lord from any dangers. Thinnan continued to stay there. His parents were worried about the sudden changes in Thinnan and wanted him back in their village. But Thinnan refused. While Thinnan was out in search of Naivedhyam for the Lord, the temple priest arrived to carry out the daily rituals to the Lord. He was shocked at the site near the Lingam, which was full of filth, the pieces of meat on the deity.

The temple priest commenced purifying work of the shrine. He performed Abhishekam of the Lord with pure water, decorated the Lingam with fresh flowers. He offered sweets and fruits as Naivedhyam and left.

Thinnan got back from hunting and found the fresh flowers, Naivedhyam, etc. He removed the entire decoration and started to worship the Lord. This practice continued for another five days. The temple priest was deeply distressed at the turn of events and prayed to the Lord.

One day, the Lord appeared in his dream and instructed him to secretly observe the worship of Thinnan. The priest arrived at the shrine and stayed behind the Lingam and observed the action of Thinnan. As usual, Thinnan came to the shrine and to his consternation, found blood oozing from the right eye of the Lingam. He cried out bitterly and tried to stop the bleeding with some herbs. But the flow of blood did not stop despite his efforts. Immediately, Thinnan plucked his right eye and fixed it on the Lingam. The bleeding stopped. Suddenly, he noticed the left eye on the Lingam had also started to bleed. He placed his foot on the exact spot where the left eye was situated on the Lingam and began to pluck his left eye with an arrow.

At this moment, a mystifying voice was heard: 'Kannappa stop plucking your eye'. Lord Shiva caught his hand and brought a sudden halt to his action. The Lord blessed Thinnan with the divine name 'Kannappa' – Who gave eyes to Lord Kannappa regained his vision. The temple priest who witnessed the whole phenomenon understood the true nature of devotion to the Lord.

The Tamil month Thai – Mrugashirsham is widely celebrated as Guru Puja day to commemorate the above incident.

The Kalahasati puranam describes that Thinnan was the son of Kunti- Arjuna in his previous birth.

Sri Kalahasti Temple

22

KARAIKKAL AMMAIYAR

Karikkal was a prosperous down in the Chola Kingdom. In this flourishing town, lived many God fearing and honest business people. Dhanadhathan was the leader of the business community. After many years of prayer, he was blessed with a charming girl child called Punithavathi. As a child she was virtuous, devout and dutiful. Punithavathi loved to hear divine stories and took keen interest in serving holy men. She had great love for Shiva. Even when she was playing with her friends, she used to utter the name of Shiva. When Punithavathi attained age, a wealthy merchant prince by name Nitipathi from Nagapattinam sought her as a bride for his son Paramadhattan.

The marriage was celebrated as per Vedic rites in grand style in the presence of many relatives and friends. After the marriage, the newly married couple stayed in Karaikkal with the bride's father providing all comforts to his only daughter.

Paramadhattan enjoyed his stay in Karaikkal with his devoted and lovely wife. The business was thriving. Punithavathi as usual spent her time praying to Shiva and found happiness in feeding the Saivite saints and giving them clothes. One day a friend of Paramadhattan gave him two mangoes. He sent it home to Punithavathi and asked her to serve it along with his lunch. A little later, a hungry Saivite saint came to her house. Punithavathi served him lunch and one mango as she did not prepare any side dishes. The old saint ate the rice and the mango and left the house after giving her blessings. After a while, her husband came for lunch. Punithavathi gave him rice, vegetable and the remaining mango fruit. The mango taste was so good, that Paramadhattan asked for the second mango. Worried that she could not comply with her husband's request, she thought of Lord Shiva for a while. Suddenly a mango fruit was placed in her hand by Divine grace. She gave the fruit to her husband who found it tastier than any other fruit. He told Punithavathi that the fruit was like ambrosia and questioned her as to the source of this wonderful mango. She narrated how she got the mango by the blessing of God. Paramadhattan refused to believe her and asked for another fruit. Punithavathi appealed to Shiva who gave her another fruit. Her husband received the fruit. Shocked and bewildered, Paramadhattan thought that his wife who received the blessings of God is a heavenly being. He also felt that it is not possible for him, an ordinary human being to live with such an evolved and saintly wife. He left home saying that he wanted to earn wealth from abroad. He went around, earned a fortune and settled in Pandyan kingdom. He married again a beautiful lady from his community. He got a female child. He named the child as Punithavathi as a respect to his first wife in Karaikkal.

Soon, Punithavathi came to know about her husband's second marriage. The relatives of Punithavathi took her to live with her husband. Paramadhattan got frightened and rushed to Punithatvathi. He fell at her feet and said aloud that she is not a human being but a Goddess. He justified his action to remarry and asked everyone to worship her.

On hearing her husband's observation, Punithavathi prayed to God to give her the form of a ghost devoid of "ephemeral beauty" of the flesh, to live her life singing in praise of Shiva. God blessed her and she obtained the form of a ghost.

Then praising the qualities of Lord Shiva, she sang "Tiruiratti –Manimalai. She then started her journey to mount Kailas. On reaching Kailas, she decided not to walk on the sacred terrain. She walked on her head and reached Lord's abode.

Shiva and Parvathi were surprised to see a fragile figure walking on her head. Sekkizhar describes the scene:

On seeing the tired and worn-out woman walking to the top of the mountain, a stunned Uma asked Shiva about the devotee approaching; When Punithavathi in the form of Ghost reached him, Shiva called her fondly" Amma". With immense joy, she fell at his feet and worshipped him. From that moment Punithivathi was known as Mother of Karaikkal (Karaikkal Ammaiyar). The Lord asked her what boon she wanted. Punithavathi appealed to God:

She pleaded with God saying that she must not have another birth and stay at HIS feet and watch the cosmic dance. Shiva granted her wish and asked her to go to Thiru Alankadu where she would see HIS dance and can remain singing about God. Seeing the celestial dance of Lord, Karaikkal Ammaiyar sang the beautiful Arpuda Thiruvanthadhi.

Karaikal Ammaiar 'Pei-Ammai' walking on her head (left) in the terrain of Kailash.

Karaikal AmmaiarTemple

Courtesy: knramesh

23

KARI NAYANAR

Kari Nayanar was a staunch devotee of Lord Shiva. He was native of Thirukadavaur. Nayanar was bestowed with a divine gift of creating amazing poems in Tamil. His elegant poetry beautifully presented with blend of fine vocabulary attracted everyone including the kings of that era namely, the Chera, the Chola and the Pandya. All the Tamil Kings appreciated and admired the rendering of Tamil Kovais (anthology) by the Nayanar. They gave him lavish gifts and plenty of money. He earned enough money to build many temples. At the same time he spent his wealth in spreading the cause of Saivism. He also served the Shivan Adiyars (devotees of Shiva_) and earned Lord's grace.

In Amirtaghatesvara temple at Thirukkadaiyur, the sculpture of Kungliyakkaliayar and Kari Nayanar are found in the the fourth Prakara northern side of Thirumaligaipathi Mandapa.

Thirukadavaur

Kari Nayanar
Illustration courtesy: Ramalingar Paini Mandram

24

KAZHARSINGA NAYANAR

Kazharsinga Nayanar was a Pallava King from the Kadava dynasty. He had the reputation of conquering many kingdoms to the North. He became an emperor. He also propagated Saivism in all the regions and visited the innumerable Shiva temples.

Once, he took a pilgrimage to Thiruvarur with his queen to shrine of Araneri dedicated to Lord. Shiva. The temple is dedicated to Sri Achaleswarar located in the Thigaraja Temple complex. The Royal couple gathered at the temple hall where varieties of flowers were gathered for making garlands and puja. As the queen entered the mantap, a flower fell from the dais where garlands were made. The queen picked up the flower and smelt it. It is said in Hinduism, that none should smell the flowers meant for God. Seruthunai Nayanar who was rendering service to the temple got annoyed at the queen and without hesitation cut off the nose of the queen that smelt the fragrance of the flower. Queen yelled in agony of the pain.

The king on hearing the loud cry of the queen, rushed to the spot. The king became furious with the Nayanar responsible for this gruesome act. The Nayanar explained to him the queen's action which was an insult to Lord Shiva.

Being a strong devotes of Shiva, the King could not bear the insult to Shiva. He gave an additional punishment by cutting off her hand which picked the flower. The devotees lauded the action of the King and Seruthunai Nayanar. At that moment the celestials rained flowers on them and they attained the grace of Lord Shiva.

Sri Achaleswarar (Vandarkuzhali) temple

25

KOCHENGAT CHOLA NAYANAR

In Chandra Thirtha in the Chola Kingdom, there was a thick grove. There was a Shiva Lingam under a Jambul tree in the grove. An elephant used to come daily and prostrate before the Lingam. A spider was also equally devoted to the God and noticed that the leaves were falling on the Lingam. The spider spun a web above lingam to prevent falling of dry leaves on the Lingam. The next day when the elephant came to worship the Lingam, he found the web and inferring that someone had polluted the sacred place, tore the web in anger, offered worship and went away. The spider came to pray and found the web has been destroyed. He wove another one and went away. Again the next day, the elephant came and started pulling the web. At that time, spider was present and in anger gave a sting. The elephant died on the spot.

The spider too was caught in the elephant's trunk and got crushed. The spider was born as the son of Suba Devan, the Chola King as ordained by Lord Shiva.

Suba Devana and his wife Kamalavati went to Chidambaram and prayed to Lord Nataraja for a son. The Lord granted their wish. Soon the queen conceived. On the day of delivery, the astrologers predicted that if the child was delivered few minutes later, it would rule the three worlds. Hearing this prophesy, the queen ordered that she should be tied to the roof upside down, with bandages around her waist. At the auspicious time, she was released and the child was born. The child had red eyes as he remained in the mother's womb for few minutes extra. The mother looking at the child with red eyes called him Kochengkannano (King with red eyes). Thus, he was named as Kochengat Cholan. When he attained proper age, the king declared and made him the new King. After severe penance, he reached the abode of Lord. Shiva.

Kochengat Cholan lived long and promoted Saivism. He built the beautiful temple at Thiruvanaikaval and installed the Shiva Lingam under the same Jumbu tree. He also built many temples and mansions for the use of Shiva devotees. He also provided fertile agricultural lands to three thousand Brahmins of Thillai for regular worship at the Chidambaram temple. Finally, he was given a special place in the abode of Shiva. His glories were sung by the famous Tamil poet Poygayar in his Kalavazhi Narpathu.

26

KOOTRUVA NAYANAR

This saint was a chieftain of Kalandai. He was a staunch devotee of Lord Shiva. Every day, he would chant Shiva Panchakshara mantra. He also took pride in serving all Shiva Bhaktas. The Lord pleased with his devotion gave him all wealth and strength. He became mighty and conquered vast lands and wealth. He had four kinds of armies- squads of elephants, speeding horses, well built chariots and well trained soldiers. As he became the supreme king, he asked the three thousand Brahmins of Thillai to crown him as King. They all refused as they owed allegiance to the Chola King. All of them, fled in defeat except one priest who stayed back to do the daily puja to Lord Nataraja. He also refused to accede to the request of the king. Kootruva Nayanar appealed to God. Shiva seeing the desperation and plea appeared before him and crowned him by placing his feet on his head. Nayanar finally attained moksha.

This Panchakshara stostram is composed by Guru Adi Shankara. The slokas describes the great divine qualities of Lord. Shiva and praises his association with the mantra "Nama Shivaya". The stostra starts with the hymn Nagendra Haraya Trilohanaya. The hymn has a powerful in-depth meaning. It praises Lord Shiva by the five lettered Panchakshari mantra

Na Ma Shi va ya

This represents the five elements namely Prithvi (earth), Jala (water), Agni (fire) Vayu (air) and Akasha (space) tattvas respectively.

नागेन्द्रहाराय त्रिलोचनाय
भस्माङ्गरागाय महेश्वराय।
नित्याय शुद्धाय दिगम्बराय
तस्मै न काराय नमः शिवाय।।1।।

Naagendra-Haaraaya Tri-Locanaaya
Bhasma-Angga-Raagaaya Mahe shvaraaya |
Nityaaya Shuddhaaya Dig-Ambaraaya
Tasmai Na_Kaaraaya Namah Shivaaya ||1||

Salutations to Lord Shiva who has fine breed of snakes as his garland. He has three eyes and his body is smeared with sacred ashes. He is every pure and eternal. He has four directions as his cloths. Salutations to Lord Shiva who is represented by the syllabus "Na". The first syllable of Panchakshara Manta "Na Ma Shi Va Ya."

27

KOTPULI NAYANAR

Kotpuli Nayanar was born in Nattiyattangudi in the Chola Kingdom. His town is now known as Tirunattiyattangudi inTanjore District. He belonged to the Vellalar caste of agricultural land owners. He was a great devotee of Lord Shiva. His name "Kotpuli" means "Ferocious tiger". He was the commander-in-chief of the Chola army.

Over the years, he had become wealthy and used all his wealth to donate "hills" of rice to Shiva temples, which were used to prepare food offerings to God.

Once, when he was called on military duty, he stored tons of rice in his house, which he instructed should be used for the Naivedya, while he was away. He conveyed his orders to all his kinsmen individually.

A famine struck Nattiyattankuti. Kotpuli's family consumed the stored rice, meant for the temple offerings, to save themselves. Kotpuli won the war and returned with many gifts from the Chola king. He was upset about the consumption of rice by his family and relatives. He decided to punish them. He invited all his kin to his house for celebration of his victory. Kotpuli ordered the doors of his mansions be closed, so his relatives could not escape and made a servant stand guard. Kotpuli killed his parents, brothers and wives for their transgression. The servant requested the master to spare the life of an infant, who had not eaten the rice and was the last heir in Kotpuli's family. Kotpuli killed the infant too, reasoning he had drunk the breast milk of a woman, who had consumed the rice. Pleased by his intense devotion, Shiva appeared before Kotpuli and said "O! Hero. Your sword has expiated the sins of all these greedy people. They shall be given salvation. You too come to Shivaloka with me". Lord Shiva also took Kotpuli to his abode.

Kotpuli is said to have given two of his daughters, Cinkati and Vannapakai to Sundarar, who reared them as their foster father. Kotpuli is worshipped in the Tamil month of Aadi. He is depicted wearing a crown, with folded hands and holding a sword in his arm.

28

KULACCHIRAI NAYANAR

Kulacchirai Nayanar was born in Manamerkudi, in the Pandyan kingdom. This place was frequently visited by Shiva Bhaktas. Kulacchirai Nayanar adored all the Shiva devotees. He considered Shiva Bhaktas equal to Lord Shiva.

Kulacchirai Nayanar was the Prime Minister of the Pandiayan King. He was the richest man in the place but did not attach any importance to wealth. He believed that wealth was the property of Shiva devotees. Gnanasambandar extolled his great qualities in one of his songs.

Nayanar helped the queen get rid of the evil influence of Jainism. He invited Samabandar to Madurai to counter the Jains attempt to influence people. Jains could not bear this and set fire to the Sambandar's camp. Unperturbed, Sambandar sang a verse and the fire was extinguished.

At that time, the Pandyan king had very high fever. The Jains could not cure the king. Sambandar applied the sacred ash on the king. Immediately the King got cured. Sambandar accepted the challenge and debate with the Jains on various points. The Jains were defeated. Kulacchirai Nayanar sent the defeated Jains to the gallows. He served Shiva devotees and finally attained Shiva's abode

Jagatheeswarar Temple, Manamelkudi...

29

KUNGILYA KALAYA NAYANAR

Kungilya Kalaya Nayanar was born in Thirukkadaiyur, Tamil Nadu. He was a very ardent devotee of Lord Amritaghateswarar and Annai Abhirami. He performed the duties of temple priest. He served the Lord by offering incense stick called Kungiliya. Hence he was called Kungiliya Nayanar. By doing his service continuously and buying the incense stick from his resources, his wealth got exhausted. He had no option but to sell his wife's sacred "Thali" to buy incense sticks at the cost of starvation of his wife and children. Lord Shiva was moved by his selfless devotion, restored his wealth.

A Shiva devotee named Thadakai was worshipping the Lord for a child. When she was about to garland the God, her sari slipped down. She managed to hold the sari but found it difficult to garland the lord. Shiva bent down to accept the garland from the devotee. From that day the deity remained in a slanted position. So the temple is known as Thadagaeeswaram and the deity as Thadagaeesaramudaiar. The slanted position of Shiva drew attention of the ruling king. The king tried to straighten it with the help of his army but failed. The king sought the help of Kalaya Nayanar. Nayanar tied a rope to his neck and to the Linga and straightened the deity to the original position. Pleased with Kalaya Nayanar, the king gave lot of wealth to Kungiliya Nayanar who spent all the wealth towards performing puja at home and in the temple. Kalaya Nayanar attained Kailash after his death.

Thirukadaiyur Temple and Goddess Abhirami

Kunguliya Nayanar gets the Shivalinga to original position by pulling it with his neck.

Thirupanandhal - Sri Arunajadeshwarar Temple

30

MAIPORUL NAYANAR

Sethiper narkoviloor malada mannar
Thiruvedam meiporulath thelentha sinthai
Neethiyanar udan poruthu thoura maaran
Nedum senam kodum padaiyum neekazaha vannam
Matharpol orumurai kondu anukee vaalal
Vunmai poorinthida marundu vantha thatthan
Kathalura namarthattha yenru nokick
Keith anal vatu iraivanai kai kondarae

Thirukovilur was the land of abundant water, fertile land where Maiporul Nayanar lived as a humble and a pious king. He was from the hill tribes of Sethi. As a brave warrior, he won many battles. He ensured that his subjects lived in happiness and prosperity. People adored him and worshipped him like a guardian angel.

Maiporular was also well versed in the Agamas. He was an ardent devotee of Shiva. He believed that Shiva and His devotees, adorned with matted locks, Rudraksham and sacred ashes represented only absolute truth. He believed in "Sarvaam Shivamayam" and saw everything with that inner vision. In his reign

Shiva Bhaktas enjoyed total freedom. Though he was a king, he devoted his time offering daily pujas, prayers. He conducted all the events in grand aura especially the temple festival. Soon Maiporul's devotion to god and his love for the people spread far and wide.

This evoked the envy of tiny little kingdoms and the rulers around his land. A king named Muthanathan close to his state became angry and arrogant and decided to wage war against Maiporular. Muthanathan gathered a huge army and continuously attacked Nayanar. He was vanquished many times. Seeing that there was no hope of winning the war, Muthunathan hatched a cunning plot. Aware of the fact that Nayanar was a dedicated devotee and could be easily fooled if he disguised as Shiva Yogi, Muthunathan in the disguise as Shiva Yogi ventured to reach the royal palace late night. The guards at the gate mistaking him as a true Shiva Yogi allowed him to proceed as the devotees of Shiva had no restriction in Nayanars kingdom.

The Shiva Yogi approached the bedroom of the king, Dathan the guard tried to dissuade him from waking up the king. Shiva Yogi turned to Dathan saying that he had some valuable Shastra to teach the king and it cannot be postponed.

Dathan became suspicious, yet allowed him to enter the bedroom of Nayanar. Suddenly Nayanar's wife got up and was surprised to see a Shiva Yogi in the bed room. She woke up her husband.

The Shiva Yogi told the king that he had come to give a great Shastra to the king and it was given by Lord Shiva. He added that the Shastra can only be given to the King and no one else. King asked the queen to be away for a while.

Shiva Yogi (Muthanathan), swiftly stabbed Nayanar on his back, with a knife he had kept hidden. At that time, Dathan, entered the room, found the king on the floor in a pool of blood and Muthanathan with a knife in his hand. He was about to kill Muthanathan, when the dying Nayanar told Dathan that a Shiva Yogi must be honoured and asked him not to harm him. Nayanar gave an order to escort Yogi to the border of his kingdom.Dathan obeyed his king. As he was escorting Muthanathan, the people who had heard the incident came to attack Muthanathan. When they were told of the king's commands, they silently withdrew, Muthanathan was safely escorted out of the kingdom, Dathan came back to convey this news to the dying king. Nayanar called all his Ministers and relatives to his bedside, and told them that it was a binding duty to serve and honour the Bhaktas. His last wish was that his kingdom is flooded with Shiva yogis and people can walk in their celestial footsteps. Nayanar closed his eyes mediating on Shiva.

Lord Shiva at that moment appeared and said how immensely pleased he was with the devotion of His Bhaktas. Even in a murderer you saw me. You are, therefore, fit to reach the Highest Abode which even the Devas cannot hope to reach. You will soon come to My Abode.

More things are wrought by prayer than these world dreams of." Alfred Lord Tennyson

The Lord is enshrined in the hearts of all
The Lord is the supreme Reality
Rejoice in him through renunciation.
Covet nothing. All belong to the Lord."
–Isha Upanishad

Faith is a force that is greater
than knowledge or power or skill,
and the darkest defeat turns to triumph
if you trust in God's wisdom and will,
For faith is a mover of mountains—

there's nothing man cannot achieve
if he has the courage to try it
and then has the faith to believe.
–Helen Steiner Rice

Thirukoilur

Thirukoilur is a small town studded with a number of temples both Vaishnava and Saiva sects. It was once a capital of an important chieftain Malayaman of Sangam age datable to 3rd century BCE to 3rd century CE. To corroborate this, a Tamil Brahmi inscription at Jambai (near Tirukkovilur) mentions about the king Athiyaman Neduman Anchi as Sathiya Puto Atiyan. Malaiyaman Tirumudikkari was the illustrious ruler of this dynasty. The Sangam works speak of the invasion of Tirukkoilur and defeat of Malayaman Tirumudikkari by Neduman Anchi, king of Takadur (modern Dharmapuri) who is said to have offered Avvaiyar, the celebrated poetess (of that period), a myrobalan (gooseberry) fruit to increase her longevity.

Thirukoilur seems to have been an important religious center as Kanchipuram in Tondaimandalam. There is ample evidence to prove that Vaishnavism, Saivism and Jainism had flourished at this center. It is said the Mudal Alvars, the first three Alvars, (Poigai, Butham and Pei) were made to meet by the grace of Almighty in one place at Thirukoilur and in ecstasy they sang poems on Ulagalanda perumal; these songs were known as Divyaprabhandam. The presiding deity of the temple Tiruvikrama Perumal is still a wooden image and this retains its ancient character.

Thirukoilur, which is also famous for Saivism, was sung by the Saiva saints as one of the Ashtavirattanams. (Dept of Archeology)

Meiporul Nayanar panel: The Nayanar is fatally wounded; the bodyguard rushes to kill the fake monk; even as he is dying, the Nayanar stops his bodyguard from attacking the murderer.

31

MANAKKANCHARA NAYANAR

Kancharur was a fertile village in Tamil Nadu where sugarcane juice and honey was abundant and flowing like a river. The village got its name from the Tamil meaning "Juice". In this village lived Manakkanchara, a pious benefactor who was devoted to God and dedicated to the service of the devotees. He was also the chief of the king's armed forces. He was wealthy, but humble. He had many men to do his bidding. Yet he served the devotees of the Lord with respect and devotion. Manakkanchara had no issues. He prayed to God and was blessed with a beautiful daughter.

She grew up with winsome manners. Soon, Manakkanchara arranged for his daughter's marriage with Eyarkone Kalikkamar. The bride and groom's family were thrilled and fixed a suitable day for the wedding. Eyarkon kalikkamar arrived in town for the wedding. Amidst the fun, frolic and music played in the marriage hall, arrived the Lord in the guise of a yogi. He wore an earring ball that swung in the air, the holy thread decorated his chest and in his hand, he held the holy ash. With His body glowing like fire, he entered the house of the devotee.

As soon as he saw the Shiva yogi, Manakkanchara fell at His feet. His joy knew no bounds for it was a good omen that a Shiva yogi graced the occasion. For the giver of boons, it was an excellent opportunity to show the world the unflinching loyalty of His devotee. After paying him due respect, Manakkanchara brought his beautiful haired daughter to pay obeisance to the sage.

The God, who obscures the 'maya' in the hearts of devotees, told Nayanar that the gorgeous hair of his daughter would be useful to make the sacred rope of hair that he wore. He wanted every strand that adorned the young girl's head. Nayanar took that statement as an order, as a boon; he immediately drew his dagger and cut off the dark pretty hair of his daughter and presented it to the sage.

The sage acted as if he accepted it and immediately disappeared only to reappear seated on the Holy Bull (rishaba) with the mother of the universe to His left amidst a rain of flowers. Nayanar prostrated, cried out of joy on seeing the divine vision and extolled the Lord.

The Lord blessed him and said that it was a deed (Thiruvilayadal) to exhibit the devotee's love for God to the world. Eyarkon, the groom arrived just then and came to know the great deed of Manakkancharar. His heart was filled with emotions of salutations to Manakkancharar.

Blessed were those eyes which witnessed the marriage of Eyarkon with the girl who got back her beautiful tresses by the grace of the God. Needless to say that Manakkanycharar got a permanent place serving at the feet of the Lord. Let the readiness of Manakkancharar Nayanar to sacrifice even at the time of his loving daughter's marriage be etched in our minds. Total surrender to His will is the only way to attain eternal bliss.

ஸ்ரீ சுக்கிரன் ஸ்தலம்

32

MANGAYARKARASIYAR

Mangayarkarasiyar was one of the 63 Nayanmars. She is one among the three women who attained this distinction. Her devotion to Lord Shiva is recorded in the hagiographic poem in Periyapuranam compiled by Sekkizhar. She also finds a mention in Thiruthoda Thogai written by Sambandar.

Koon Pandyan, the Pandyan king was ruling in Madurai. He was hunch back. He loved Tamil and Tamil poets and established a Tamil Sangam. His wife Mangayarkarasiyar was the daughter of a Chola King. She was an ardent devotee of Lord Shiva. Kulacchirai Nayanar, a devotee of Lord Shiva was the minister in the kingdom.

Koon Pandyan favoured Jainism in his kingdom and encouraged them. This approach of the king perplexed the queen and the minister. They felt that unless a drastic action was initiated, Saivisam would be wiped out. When Sambandar came for a visit to Madurai, he preferred to stay outside the city. Kulacchirai Nayanar invited him to come to the city. The Jains tried to dissuade Sambandar from coming into the city but could not succeed. Sambandar saw the hunchback King and sang a pathigam. The king got rid of his hunchback and stood tall. He understood the power of Saivism and of Lord Shiva. After sometime, the king defeated the northern kings at Tirunelveli and spread Saivism there. Mangayarkarasiyar and her husband worshipped Sambandar with great devotion and affection. Gnana Sambandar sung pathigams in praise of both:

Madurai Meenashi Temple

33

MUNAIYADAVAR NAYANAR

Munaiyadavar Nayanar was born in Thirunidur in the Chola Kingdom. Nidur also known as Needur is on the banks of river Cauvery in Nagapattinam district, Tamil Nadu. His name literally means "he who fights the war." Though a brave soldier, he was a very staunch devotee of Lord Shiva. He used to fight for the weak and fragile kings. He utilized the enormous wealth he got to renovate ancient temples and build new ones for Lord Shiva. He ensured that regular pujas were conducted at various temples.

Munaiyadavar was born in Needur. He belonged to the Vellalar caste. He was known for his skill in handling all kinds of weapons and also tried the new ones. He fought many battles with success. His bakthi towards Lord Shiva and his service to devotees were praised by Sundarar. He praised the brave bold Nayanar in his Thiruthonda Thogai. Even today Munaiyadavar is worshipped in the Somanathaswami Temple in Needur. A shrine is dedicated to the Nayanar in the temple.

He lived long and Lord Shiva appeared before him and took him to Kailas.

Somanathaswami Temple,Needur, Mayiladuthurai/River Cauvery

34

MURKHA NAYANAR

Murkha was born in Thiruverkadu, near Chennai. He was a Vellalar, a caste of agricultural land owners. He was a great devotee of Lord Shiva. He was a ruffian and a gambler, as his name suggests, and would raise his sword whenever he encountered dishonesty or treachery.

However, Murkha Nayanar cultivated devotion to Shiva, from childhood. He used to prepare the rice with ghee, and various sweet and savory delicacies, and feed Shiva devotees. The saint spent all his wealth feeding the devotees. He sold all his possessions, including his properties and his slaves. Murkha's desire to continue to feed the devotees led him to undertake a long travel across Tamil Nadu. He visited every gambling house in every town. He came to Tirukkudanthai (Kumbakonam), the home of numerous Shiva Temples. He went to the gambling houses of the town to earn money to take care of the devotees of the blue throated Lord.

Murkha Nayanar strategically lost money in the initial stages, forcing the opponents to stake more money in the later rounds. Then, he would win all the money. He stabbed his rivals who tried to cheat. He used all the money earned, to feed the devotees of Shiva. He would never take his food till the last devotee finished his meal. This is described in the Periya Puranam by Sekkizhar.

> He would lose in the initial play and make his rival
>
> Gain money; but in all subsequent play
> He would repeatedly win and come by great money;
> He would stab them with his sword that tried to cheat
> Him with deceptious words; thus he, the good gambler,
> Came to be known as Moorkar in this fourfold world.

He lived his life gambling and serving devotees. Finally, he reached Kailas, the abode of Shiva by dint of his devotion. His relentless service expiated him from his sins.

Sri Vedapureeswarar Temple Thiruverkadu

Sri Karumari Amman temple

35  

MURTHY NAYANAR

Pandyan was an ancient Tamil dynasty. It is one of the three in Tamilnadu, the other two being Chola and Chera dynasties. The three empires ruled parts of South India around 600 BC. They ruled their country 'Pandya Nadu' from Korkai, the then seaport located at the southernmost tip of Indian Peninsula and later moved to Madurai. The Pandian Empire was a home to temples, including the famed Meenashi Amman Temple, located on the bank of Vaigai River in Madurai. The temple is dedicated to Parvathi known as Meenakshi and her consort Shiva, known here as Sundareswarar.

The Pandiyan kingdom was famous for developing literature in Tamil by having a Sangam. Housed in the temple, the Sangam bards who dwelt there raised the Tamil language to newer heights. Lord Shiva was pleased with the scintillating Tamil music and poets and devotees who spread Saivism by singing praise of the Lord.

In this fertile, flourishing city of happiness, it was a common sight to see pretty damsels adorned with lustrous pearls, brought from the deep sea by the brave seafarers of the Pandya dynasty. At dawn, the serene city of Madurai reverberated with the gentle breeze which carried the melodies of hymns dedicated to Sundareswarar and Meenakshi. The city was drowned in divinity, where hundreds of devotees spent their time in the service to the God and Goddess of the land.

Among the many Shiva devotees, there lived a rich and pious merchant called Murthi Nayanar. He religiously took the task of preparing sandal paste with his own hands and offering to the Lord. Done with utmost sincerity, the sandal paste had a unique fragrance and was famous. He did this duty without a break.

Suddenly, a Vaduka king from the north killed the Pandyan king in a battle and captured the kingdom. The new ruler was a lover of Jainism. He tortured the devotees of Lord Shiva, including Murthi Nayanar. The King's hatred did not deter Murthi Nayanar who continued his daily duty of preparing the sandal paste. The king infuriated by the faith and determination of Murthi Nayanar, blocked the entire route through which he obtained sandal. Murthiar could not get the sandal to grind. Heartbroken, yet not cowed down by the Kings atrocities, Nayanar proceeded to grind the sandal paste with his elbow on the stone used for grinding. With the skin peeled bones and nerves protruding, the blood came out causing unbearable pain.

Lord Shiva seeing the devotee's action ordered him to stop immediately. He declared that the king would be dead soon and that he would rule the kingdom. Dazed, Nayanar stood up with all his wounds healed miraculously. He sang in praise of Lord Shiva. The very next day, the king died without leaving an heir. The ministers were perplexed and decided to solve the issue. They sent the state elephant round the town with a garland to choose the successor to the throne.

The elephant blind folded, entered the temple and placed the garland around Murthy Nayanar's neck. The majestic elephant saluted Nayanar and placed him on its back and hurried to the palace. The city folks gathered and cheered their new king. On reaching the palace, Murthi Nayanar summoned ministers and said "if the fragrance of Saivism spreads, then I am ready to rule the country". All of them conceded to the request and considered it as a boon. He further said that even if he becomes the king, he would have only holy ash as the sandal, rudraksha as the valuable ornament and matted hair as the crown. As a king, he therefore donned Rudraksha beads, smeared his body with sacred ash and sported the matted hair. He was hence fondly praised as 'mummaiyal ulakanda murthiyar' (nayanar who ruled the world with three holy things). Murthi Nayanar ruled wisely till he attained salvation at the fragrant feet of Shiva.

Murthy Nayanar: Giving his own body for the cause of Shiva

Meenashi Amman Temple, Madurai.

36

MURUGA NAYANAR

Kathalakee kasinthu kannere mulgi
Oothuvar thamai nanneeri kuipathu
Veda nankeenu meiporulavathu
Naathanama Namashivayavae..
Sambandar
Those who repeat it while love's tear outpour
It gives them life, and guides them in the way
'Tis the true substance of the Vedas four
The Lord's great name, wherefore ' Hail
Shiva'(Namashivaya) say..

Pugar also known as Poompugar is a town in Nagapattinam district, in the southern Indian state of Tamil Nadu. It was once a flourishing ancient port city known as Cauvery Poompattinam, and for a while served as the capital of the early Chola kings in Tamilakam. Pugar is located near the end point of the Cauveri River, beside the sea coast. Pugar is the place where the Tamil Yogi Thirunavukkarasar attained Shiva Samadhi.

Muruga Nayanar was born in Pumpukalur/Thirupukalur, one of the most prosperous lands in Chola Kingdom. He was born in a family of Vedic scholars. He was an ardent devotee of Lord Shiva – Lord Agnishwara. He worshipped Lord Shiva with the flowers of enthralling fragrances.

Getting up before Sun rise, with only the thought of the Lord, he would wander around the forests in the hills procuring fragrant flowers. He would wade through ponds to get lotus and pick different varieties of fresh flowers from creepers. From the huge collection of assorted flowers and fragrance, he would separate the good and flawless flowers and collect them in different baskets. At the temple, Muruga Nayanar would sit alone, and make attractive floral garlands and a crown and offer it to Vardhamaneswarar (Shiva), the presiding deity. The Lord Vardhamaneswarar whose feet are softer than the petals of rose enjoyed the service of this sincere devotee. The Nayanar spent his time in meditating on Shiva and sang Thevaram hymns. He also spent his time in serving Shiva devotees.

Muruganar had the boon of being a friend of Thirugnana Sambandar and old sage Thirunavukkrasar. Muruga Nayanar compassionately received these two holy men with honour to his home in Pumpukalur.

Sambandar was greatly impressed by the devotion of Muruga Nayanar and offered his blessing and visited him often to enjoy his hospitality. Muruga Nayanar's affection for Sambandar was so great that he could not bear separation from the great devotee of Shiva.

Muruga Nayanar took part in the grand wedding of Sambandar at Nallur. During the wedding, a divine light suddenly shone and the entire venue was suffused with its brilliance. Sambandar disappeared in the light and Murganar too entered the effulgent flame, chanting the name of Shiva.

Cauveryi Poompattinam

37

NAMI NANDI ADIGAL

Nami Nandi Adigal was born in a small town Emapperur near Thiruvarur. The town was part of the Chola Kingdom. Nami was a bramin and belonged to the priest caste. He was a staunch devotee of Lord Shiva. He used to go to the shrine Araneri in Thirvarur and perform routine pujas and lighting of lamps.

One day he wanted to light all the lamps in the temple which is an act highly extolled in the Shiva Agamas. Nandi Adigal approached a Jain in the nearby house of the temple and asked for some ghee to light the lamps. The Jain stoutly refused to give ghee and ridiculously suggested that Nayanar light the temple lamps with water. Humiliated Nayanar appealed to the Lord and expressed his helplessness. At once a voice asked him to go to the temple tank and get water and light the lamps. Nandi Adiagal lit all the temple lamps with the water and the entire vicinity of the temple became bright and radiant. The Jains were amazed to witness such a miracle. The routine of lighting the lamp with water continued and became the talk of the town. Few Jains embraced Saivism.

The news of the marvel reached the ears of the King. Pleased with the Naynars dedication, the king appointed him as the head of the temple. Nami Nayanar used to celebrate the Panguini Uttaram (annual festival) in magnificent manner which attracted hundreds of devotees. During the festival, the Lord would be taken to a place called Tirumanali where people of all castes come to worship the Lord. On this occasion Nandi Adigal came home after doing rituals but felt that the other castes had polluted him. So he did not enter the house to do his daily puja. He asked his wife to bring some water so that he could bathe to ward off the pollution and then enter the house. But he was tired and overpowered by sleep. In his dream Lord appeared and told him all those who came for the festival and born inThiruvarur are my servants (Ganas) and there is no disparity. Adigal woke up from sleep and informed his wife about the dream. He performed his worship. In the morning, he went to Thiruvarur and saw the same form as God himself. Adigal prostrated before them all. It was the Lila of god to make him realize that all are the same with faith in God. Nandi Adigal served the Lord and his devotees so nicely that Appar praised him as "Anipon" (Pure gold). In the course of time, Adigal reached Kailas with glory.

Nami Nandi Adigal: lights the oil lamps of the temple with water

38

NARASINGA MUNIYARAIYAR

Narasinga Muniyaraiyar was a petty chieftain. He lived in Tirumunaipadi. He was highly devoted to Lord Shiva. He was a champion of Saivism. He was a contemporary of Sundarar and almost like a foster parent to him. The saint lived at Tirunavalur (Tirunamanullur). People lived happily during his reign.

On every Tiruvathirai star (Arudra nakshtra) day, he would conduct special Puja, feed Shiva devotees in whatever form they appeared and offer a gift of a hundred gold coins to each. On this auspicious day, the devotees were fed well and at the end of the feast, he would liberally distribute gold coins.

One fine day, God decided to test Muniyaraiyar. God has chosen the specific day of Arudhra to reveal the faith and devotion of Narasinga Muniyaraiyar. On one such Thiruvathirai day, a man who was not a devotee of Shiva, but a trickster, attended the puja with holy ash smeared all over his naked body. His presence was resisted by the other devotees. Instead of developing detestation at the nudity, Muniyaraiyar gave a respectful welcome by prostrating before him and served the royal banquet with full hospitality. The chieftain also extended 200 gold coins to the devotee. The reverence and respect shown by Narasinga Muniyaraiyar earned the benign grace of Shiva and the saint was liberated from the cycle of rebirth. The hypocrite, on his part, felt small and thereafter lived a reformed life.

In the Tamil month of Puratassi, Sadayam star, shatabhishak is celebrated as Guru Puja day of Narasinga Muniyaraiyar Nayanar.

The King Named Vanangamudi Muniyaraiyar is mentioned in Tamil Copper Plate Inscriptions. He is also mentioned by Kalki in his book 'Ponniyin Selvan'. He mentioned that Vanangamudi Muniyaraiyar was one of the Petty Kings comparable with Pazhuvettaraiyar, Malavarayar (Malayaman), Sambuvarayar. These kings held positions of power and influence under the Cholas and were related to the royal family by marriage.

Tirunavalur temple

39

NESA NAYANAR

Nesa Nayanar was a native of Kumbilli. He was a weaver by profession. He was a dedicated devotee of Lord Shiva. He always uttered the Panchakshara Mantra. He used to always chant "Om Namashivaya" from dawn to dusk. He was generous in donating cloths and food to all Shiva devotees. He firmly believed that offering food and clothes to devotees is the best service to God.

Till his death, he continued to chant Lord's name and served the devotees. After his death, Nayanar reached holy abode of Kailas.

Kumbilli

40

NINRA SEER NEDUMARA NAYANAR

Thiru Alavai/Madurai was ruled by King Kunpandiyan and his wife Mangaiyarkarasiyar. Kunpandiyan patronized Jainism and embraced Jain teachings and philosophies. The queen was a staunch devotee of Lord Shiva. The king prohibited the worship of Lord Shiva and practice of Saiva Siddhanta. Queen Mangaiyarkarasiyar was rattled and anticipated a substantial damage to the Shiva worship and trouble to the devotees of Shiva.

Mangaiyarkarasiyar approached her minister Kulachiraiyar who was also a Shiva devotee. Both invited Gnana Sambandar's to Madurai with the intention of reinstating the faith in Shiva and curb Jainism from spreading in their kingdom. Gnana Sambandar's stayed outside the city to avoid confrontation with the Jains. At the behest of queen, Sambandar's consented to visit the King. At that time, the king was suffering from agonizing pain due to his hunchback and severe blisters. Seeing the pitiable state of the king, Sambandar's passionately sung few hymns in praise of Lord Shiva. Sambandar's prayer had an instant impact on the king. His hunchback vanished and he stood tall. He was then called Ninraser Nedumara Nayanar.

Nayanar saw the miracle happened to him and became a dedicated servant of Lord Shiva. He travelled with his queen the length and breadth of his kingdom and spread Saivism. Kulaichirai Nayanar also accompanied them in the mission to firmly spread Saivisam. Finally all attained the abode of Lord Shiva.

https://earthcelebrations.com/vaigai-river

41

PERUMIZHALAI KURUMBA NAYANAR

Perumizhalai Kurumba Nayanar was born in Perumizhalai village (Perumanallur and Devamala), located in Pudukottai. He was born in a Kurumba family (shepherd community) and engaged in feeding the flocks by extensive grazing and weaving their wool into shawls.

Kurumba Nayanar was a servant of Shivaperuman, a chieftain who governed the Perumizhalai region. The saint used to pack sufficient food and other articles in a woolen cloth and forward them from the border of the region. The Nayanar was noted for his simple nature and austerity by the people. The saint spent his life in great devotion and faith.

Kurumba Nayanar was a contemporary of Sundarar. He was also his admirer and accepted him as his guru. Kurumba Nayanar excelled in Guru Bhakti. He was an ardent devotee of Lord Shiva and Shiva Bhaktas, too. To him, Sundarar was the sole refuge. He adored the Guru in thought, word and deed. By the Guru's grace, he attained all the Siddhis. He was immersed in Shiva Bhakti and Guru Bhakti.

Sundarar proceeded to the sacred land of Thiruvanchikulam on a spiritual journey. Using his siddhis,

Kurumba Nayanar came to know that Shiva had decided to recall Sundarar to His divine abode, by granting Sundarar salvation. As the troubled Kurumba Nayanar felt that he could not live without his beloved guru, he left his mortal body with his ashta siddhis and yogic powers. The saint enjoyed chanting Panchakshara as well as the hymns of Thiruthonda Pathikam. Thiruthonda Pathikam is part of Thiruthonda Thogai composed by Sundarar in praise of the 63 Nayanars. Sundarar has mentioned about Perumizhalai, in his Vaippu Sthalangal in Tevaram.

All his inner organs became one; pure consciousness
Streamed through suzhu-manai; by cultivated yoga
Pranava caused the opening of Brahmarantra;
Through this his spirit coursed its way to the Kailas
To the feet of the Primal One even before Nampi Aroorar
Could there arrive. (Translation by T. Ramachandran)

Tamil month Adi – Chithirai star is widely celebrated as Guru Puja Day of Kurumba Nayanar. The guru Puja of Perumizhalai Kurumba Nayanar is celebrated every year in his home town.

*Ashta siddhis are mentioned in Patajanli's Yoga Sutras and can be obtained by very few, through countless years of practice and devotion to all the eight limbs of Ashtanga Yoga. Siddhi can loosely be translated as accomplishment or a special power or unusual skill. The eight siddhis are:

Anima : Reducing one's physical self to the size of an atom

Mahima : Growing one's physical self to an incredibly large size

Garima : Making one's physical self so heavy as immovable by others

Laghima : Becoming almost weightless

Prapti	:	Being able to go/travel wherever one wants
Prakamya	:	Being able to obtain whatever one wants
Istva	:	Possessing lordship
Vastva	:	Being able to control the minds of others

Perumizhalai God and goddess

42

PUGAL CHOLA NAYANAR

Pugal Chola Nayanar was an early Chola king. Uraiyur was the place where he lived. He is described as the ancestor of Kulothunga Chola II. Pugal Chola Nayanar was an ardent devotee of Lord Shiva and his devotees.Pugal Chola was an ideal monarch who served his subjects, Shiva and devotees of Shiva. Saivism prospered under his reign. He was the emperor of the region and had numerous vassals.

Once, he visited Karuvur, which was one of the chief towns of the Chola kingdom. As already told in the story of Eripatta Nayanar, this is the king who offered to have his head severed for the cause of justice, when his state elephant scattered the flowers of Sivakami Andar kept for puja.

While in Karuvur, the Chola king learnt that a vassal prince named Adigan (Adiyaman) was due to pay tributes to the king. The king declared war on the vassal and ordered his troops to destroy the enemy fort. The Chola army triumphed. Adigan escaped death, by abandoning his citadel. The Chola warriors arrived with the wealth and women from Adigan's city and brought severed heads of their fallen foes as a sign of valour. As the king surveyed the pile of heads, he saw a head with matted hair. On investigation, he realized his soldiers had killed a Shaiva ascetic. To expiate the sin of killing a devotee of Shiva, he decided to end his life. He crowned his son as the king. He built a funeral pyre. He smeared his body with sacred ash and took the head of the devotee in a golden, jewel-studded vessel on his head. He circumambulated the blazing flames, reciting the Panchakshara mantra to placate Shiva and plunged into the fire. For his supreme sacrifice, he attained Kailas, after his death. A holy day in his honour is observed in the Tamil month of Adi, where the moon enters the Krittika Nakshtra (lunar mansion).

Panchavarnswamy Temple is locates in Tamil Nadu, is about 2000 years old. Panchavarnasamy Temple is a famous Shiva temple. It is believed that Shiva depicts five different colours (panchaputhas), hence the name Panchavarnasamy. Panchavarnasamy is a famous place where the 7th century Tamil Hindu spiritual works were sung by Nayanars.

43

PUGAZH TUNAI NAYANAR

The Nayanar was Adi Saiva of Sriviliputhur. He was a Shiva devotee and priest of the temple. His routine was to bathe the deity, chanting mantras and perform the puja according to the Shiva Agamas.

Once a great famine swept the area which resulted in starvation and lack of food. Nayanar had no money to buy food. He had no mind to leave the temple and continued to do his puja though it was a strain and pain to him. He was exhausted. Yet he fetched some water in a pot and tried bathe (abhishekam) the deity. As he was pouring the water on the Lingam, the pot slipped out of his hand. He also fainted and fell asleep due to fatigue

The Lord appeared in his dream and told him that he would leave one coin in the temple everyday till the famine is over so that he could buy food and appease his hunger and also do his duty. Nayanar woke up and found the dream was true. He found the coin daily and happily continued to do his puja. Finally, he reached the abode of God.

44

PUSALAR NAYANAR

Pusalar also known as Pusalar Nayanar is an eighth-century devotee venerated in Saivisam. He is counted as the fifth-eighth in the list of 63 Nayanars His hagiography speaks how he created a grand temple for Shiva in his mind and how his patron god Shiva preferred attending the consecration of his mind temple, instead of a grand temple created by a Pallava king.

Pusalar was a Brahmin of Tiruninravur in Thondai Mandalam. He excelled in the mental worship of the Lord. He strongly desired to build a temple for Lord Shiva, but he did not have the money for it. So, mentally he gathered the necessary materials for the purpose. He laid the foundation stone. He raised the temple and had even fixed an auspicious day for the installation of the deity in it.

The Kadava king who was also a great devotee of Lord Shiva had built a magnificent temple in Kanjeevaram. By chance he had also fixed the date which Pusalar had mentally chosen, for the installation of the Lord in his temple. The Lord wanted to show the king the superiority of Pusalar's great devotion. Shiva appeared in the king's dream and asked him to postpone the installation ceremony in his temple, as He would be going to the temple constructed by

His devotee at Tiruninravur. The king woke up from sleep and wanted to have the Darshan of the devotee. The King also desired to have a look at the great temple he had built, which he thought would be far superior to his temple.

The king came to Tiruninravur and found no big temple in existence. Then, he found out Pusalar's house and approached him. Pusalar was stunned when he heard of the king's dream. Soon, he recovered and was filled with joy. He thought: 'How kind and merciful is the Lord. I am only a wretched creature and He has accepted my mental shrine as His Abode. I am really blessed.' He told the king that the temple was only in his mind. The king was surprised to hear this. Admiring Pusalar's devotion, the king fell at his feet and worshipped him. Pusalar installed the Lord in his mental temple and continued to worship Him till he attained His Abode.

The Hirudayaleeswarar ("Lord in Devotees' heart") was built in Thiruninravur by the Pallavas in honour of Pusalar. Pusalar is worshipped with Shiva in the sanctum sanctorium of the temple. As per temple lore, this temple was created by the Pallava king from Pusalar's tale to fulfill Pusalar's wish to build a grand temple for Shiva. Since Pusalar originally built the temple in his heart, patients of heart diseases as well as cardiologists worship at this temple for cure of heart diseases. A holy day in his honour is observed on the twenty-eighth day of Aippasi, which generally coincides with November 13

Pusalar Nayanar
Illustration courtesy: Ramalingar Paini Mandram

45

RUDRA PASUPATHI NAYANAR

Naagendra-Haaraaya Tri-Locanaaya
Bhasma-Angga-Raagaaya Mahe shvaraaya
Nityaaya Shuddhaaya Dig-Ambaraaya
Tasmai Nakaaraaya Namah Shivaaya

(Salutations to Him): Who has the King of Snakes as His Garland and Who has Three Eyes,
Whose Body is Smeared with Sacred Ashes and Who is the Great Lord,
Who is Eternal, Who is ever Pure and Who has the Four Directions as His Clothes,
Salutations to that Shiva, Who is represented by syllable "Na",
Panchakshara mantra"

Sri Rudram is a Hindu stotra dedicated to Rudra (Shiva), taken from the Yajurveda. The text is also famous for its mention of the "namah shivaya" mantra. Chanting the Rudram is considered to be of immense benefit. Legend says that Lord Shiva after Bhasmasura was killed with the help of Vishnu performed Tandava dance and then chanted "Rudra Yagna" at the venue where Sri Kalahasti Temple exists today.

Sri Rudram, also known as Rudraprasna, comprises of two parts. The first part is known as Namakam The second part is known as Chamakam. It is one of the most sacred and powerful Vedic hymns and is recited in pujas and homam by Vedic pundits for all round benefits. Foremost among the mantras contained in Rudram is the Panchakshari Mantra.

On the banks of the rich river Cauvery, there were many fertile villages full of vast lush green paddy fields, groves, forests known for its scenic beauty. The natural beauty of the lands on the bank of the river Cauvery created a unique atmosphere of divinity. There was a small village called Tiruttalaiyur. Here, Brahamins lit a sacrificial fire which rose up to heaven. The dense forests with wonderful, varied fragrant flowers lured the honey bees which provided plenty of honey for abhishekham of Shiva. The cows which consumed the rich green grass produced copious milk for the abhishekam of the dancing Shiva.

Rudra Pasupathi Nayanar was born in Tiruttalaiyur in a Brahmin family of Vedic scholars. The Nayanar was a fervent devotee of Shiva. He made it a practice of chanting the Sri Rudram regularly.

Each morning at sunrise, he would get into the very cold lotus lake. He would stand in water up to his neck. With folded hands above his head, he would start chanting Rudram in a clear accent. Pasupathi, found immense pleasure in praising Lord Rudra by chanting the Shiva Panchakshara Mantra.

He would repeat the chant in the afternoon, evening and night without fail. His regular, faultless and systematic chants pleased the Lord. He always felt close to the feet of dancing Shiva. He was soon recognized as Rudra Pasupthiyar. On a fine day, pleased and lured by his uninterrupted chanting, Shiva blessed Rudra Pasupathi Nayanar. Nayanar attained the abode of Lord Shiva. In the Tamil month of Purratasi, Ashwini star, the day is widely celebrated as Guru Puja day in Thiruthalayur.

46

SADYANAR

Sadyanar lived in Tirunavalur in Tirumuraipadi. All his ancestors were Shiva devotees. Sadyanar was also pious and devoted to God. His wife Isaignaniyar was also devotee of Shiva and a dutiful wife. The couple were totally devoted to God and a divine and noble child was born to them.

Narasinga Munaiyar, the king happened to see the child and was astounded by the beauty (Tejas). He made a request that he should be allowed to bring up the child. The parents seeing the genuine love and affection of the king handed over the child to him. They led the ideal Grihasta life and finally attained the abode of God

Tirunavalur

47

SAKKIYA NAYANAR

I am a serviteur of Saakkiyan who unforgettingly
Pelted the ankleted feet of the Lord of Uma-- the Lady
Of lovely breasts covered by a breast-band."
–The Tiru-th-Tonda-th-Tokai.

Sakkiya Nayanar, one of the 63 saints, was from Tirucchangamangai, a village in Tamil Nadu. He was born in an aristocratic agricultural family. He was a Vellalar, a caste of agricultural land owners. He gave up worldly life and studied in pursuit of the truth to attain moksha (emancipation). He was sent to Kanchipuram to study Buddhism and realize the truth. He lived with Buddhist monks, in the university in Kanchipuram. He earned the name Sakkiya, originating from Shakya - the clan of the Buddha. However, Buddhism did not relinquish his thirst for knowledge and enlightenment. So, he embraced Shaivism. He did not give up the garb of a Buddhist monk. He continued to dress in saffron garments as he was convinced that external appearance did not matter for self-realization.

He studied secretly Saiva Siddhantam and found that 'Shiva Jnana' could take him to the truth. Sakkiya commenced the worship of the Lingam.

One day, he unconsciously threw a stone at the lingam

with great devotion. The next day, Sakkiya felt that it was Shiva's divine wish that he worship, by throwing a stone a day, at the lingam as an offering. Every day, he went to a street temple before taking his food, and flung stones towards the Shiva Linga as if they were flowers! Because of his devout intention, Shiva accepted these stones as flowers.

Sakkiya realized that God will accept any offering, if done with great devotion. Sakkiya would not have food without throwing a stone at the lingam daily. Once, Sakkiya forgot his daily stone worship and was about to partake food. Suddenly, he remembered his daily duty and unmindful of hunger, rushed to the temple and threw a pebble at the lingam.

The monks understood the ways of Sakkiya Nayanar and rushed towards him with swords to kill him. Sakkiya Nayanar clung to Shiva Linga and prayed intently. Shiva came with his bhuta ganas, fought the monks and took him to His Abode Kailas.

One devotee later sang like this:
O Shiva, one fellow flung kal (stone) at you,
Another fellow used vil (bow and arrow) at you,
One another, flung sol (angry words) at you
A fourth fellow used pal (teeth) for your worship
O! You graced them; no doubt, people call you a madcap!
On His young bull as the Lord appeared before him
The sacred serviteur folded his hands and fell
Prostrate on the ground in adoration; casting
His looks of grace on him, The Lord blessed him
With the company of the hoary serviterus in Shiva- loka.
This done, the Lord disappeared.

Sakkiya Nayanar is depicted with a top-knot or flowing matted hair and with folded hands (Anjali mudra). Anjali mudra is performed by pressing the palms of the hands together. The fingers are together with fingertips pointing up. The hands are pressed together firmly and evenly. In the common form of anjali mudra, the hands are held at the heart chakra with thumbs resting lightly against the sternum.

A holy day in his honour is observed, on the twenty-sixth day of Margazhi which coincides with January 10. The moon enters the lunar mansion on this day. He receives collective worship as part of the 63 Nayanars.

Saakkiya Nayanar: Illustration courtesy: Ramalingar Paini Mandram

48

SATTI NAYANAR

Satti Nayanar is also known as Shakti Nayanar or Sathiyar. He was a Vellala by caste. He was born in Varinjiyur in the Chola Kingdom, where river Cauvery was flowing. He was a sincere devotee of Lord Shiva and honored His devotees. He always uttered the name of Shiva and could not brook anyone speaking against his favorite God Shiva. He always carried a pair of tongs and a sharp knife in his upper towel. When he saw any man speaking against Lord Shiva, he would catch hold of him, pull out his tongue with his tongs and cut it. Those who were not Shiva devotees, were scared to go anywhere near the temples. Lord Shiva recognized his complete devotion and showered blessings and took him to Kailas.

This simple story has a moral message- that we should not speak ill, revile or disparage holy men and devotees of God. Dr. Dennis Hudson, of World Religions at Smith College has identified twenty four Nayanars including Satti Nayanar. The Professor says that Satti Nayanar's violence is justified by the maxim, "the sins of the devotees of the Lord are virtues whereas even good actions performed by those without love are vices". The Nayanar is also excused since the narrative blames the victim to be the instigator of the attack by his actions. (Source WP).

Satti Nayanar is depicted in a stone panel in the Airavatesvar temple, the 12th century Shiva Temple in Darasuram built by Raja Raja Chola II. The panel shows him cutting the tongue. A shrine in his honour was built in Varinjiyur. This Nayanar is worshipped in the Tamil month of Aippasi when the moon crosses into the Pushya nakshatra.

Airavatesvar temple, Darasuram

49

SERUTHUNAI NAYANAR

Seruthunai Nayanar, also known as Seruthunai was born in Thanjavur, Marukal Nadu, which was then part of the Pallava kingdom ruled by Kazharsinga. Kazharsinga Nayanar was also an ardent devotee of the Lord. He was a Pallava monarch, belonging to the family of Kadavar. Due to God's grace, he defeated the kings of the North Country and established Saivism there. He went on many pilgrimages.

Seruthunai belonged to the Vellalar caste of agricultural land owners. He was a devotee of Shiva. He journeyed to Thiruvaur and worshipped at the shrine of Araneri, dedicated to Shiva. This temple is identified as the Sri Achaleswarar (Vandarkuzhali) temple, located in the Thyagaraja temple complex. He volunteered to perform various services in the temple.

Once, king Kazharsinga and his queen arrived to pay respects to Shiva. The queen arrived in the temple hall where various flowers were gathered to make floral offerings to Shiva as well as garlands for him. A flower had fallen from the dais. The queen picked the flower and smelt it. In Hinduism, it is taboo to use or smell flowers meant for God, before they are offered to him.

Seruthunai Nayanar was enraged by the conduct of the Pallava queen. He dragged the queen by her hair and pushed her on the ground. He caught her nose and punished her by severing it.

The king, hearing the pitiable cry of the queen, rushed to the spot. He was terribly angry with the man who was responsible for the brutal act. Seruthunai Nayanar explained to him the queen's action which was an insult to Lord Shiva (Shiva Aparadham). The king at once gave an additional punishment to her, by cutting off her hand which picked up the flower!

Both the king and Seruthunai Nayanar were glorified by the people and the celestial rained flowers on them. Both of them attained the grace of Lord Shiva. Sundarar (8th century) venerates Seruthunai Nayanar in the Tiruthonda Thogai, a hymn to Nayanar saints. Seruthunai Nayanar is worshipped in the month of Avani.

Thanjavur temple

50

SIRAPPULI NAYANAR

I am also a serviteur of Sirappuli, the patron
of celebrated glory. Tiruthtondatokai...

Sirappuli Nayanar was a saint, venerated in the Hindu sect of Saivism. He is generally counted as the thirty-fifth in the list of 63 Nayanars. Sirappuli Nayanar is described to have served the devotees of Lord Shiva and also worshipped the Lord with various ritual practices.

Sirappuli Nayanar was born in Thiruvakkur, Nagapattinam district in Tamil Nadu. Thiruvakkur was part of the Chola kingdom and famous for its generous Brahmins. Sirappuli was one of them. His family was associated with memorizing and chanting the Vedas. He would chant the panchaakshara as ordained, foster the triple fire and make good sacrifices.

For the glory of the feet of the blue-throated Lord;
Unto the flawless devotees, he would in love that never
Suffered diminution, give bountifully
And munificently; in due time he reached the feet
Of the Lord to flourish there forever.
(Trans: Ramachandar)

Sirappuli Nayanar used to donate generously. He is praised as a "munificent giver" and called a "nimbus which rained wealth". Sambandar praises him in his Thevaram thus: "if anybody in the world out of poverty asks for something, without saying a, the generous people of Thiruvakkaur readily help them".

Following the tradition and culture of the town, Sirappuli welcomed the devotees of Shiva to his home and spoke sweet words to his guests. He used to feed them and present them with gifts. Sirappuli regularly recited the Panchakshara mantra, dedicated to Shiva. He performed many yajans in honour of Shiva.

The saint also used to smear the sacred ash on his body. He spent his days serving Shiva and his devotees, and finally attained his divine abode kailash after death. According to Shivananda Saraswati, the legend of Sirappuli Nayanar conveys the greatness of the Panchakshara mantra of Shiva and the glory of Japa.

Sirappuli Nayanar is associated with the Sri Thanthondreeswarar temple of his home town Thiruvakkur. A legend tells that the Nayanar vowed to feed a thousand devotees every day. Once, Shiva himself came as the thousandth devotee to complete the number. Thus, the icon of the temple is called Ayirathil Oruvar ("one in a thousand"). Some versions of the legend replace Sirappuli with the Chola king and Nayanar Kocengannan, who is credited as the builder of the temple.

The tale of Sirappuli Nayanar is carved in the Airavateswara Temple. Airavatesvara Temple the 12th-century Shiva temple in Darasuram built by the Chola king Raja Raja Chola II. Sirappuli Nayanar is worshipped in the month of Karthigai, when the moon enters the lunar mansion. He receives collective worship as part of the 63 Nayanars.

Shiva temple in Darasuram

51

SIRUTHONDA NAYANAR

Siruthonda Nayanar was a Brahmin, living in a small village, in the Cauvery River region. He was well versed in Sanskrit literature, the Vedas, Ayurveda and in the art of war. His original name was Paramjyoti. The Chola King, on knowing his versatility made him the commander in chief of his army. Paramjyoti went to Vatapi, for a war against the Chalukya King. He defeated the king and came back with a Ganapati statue, called Vatapi Ganapati.

When the Chola king was wondering about Paramjyoti's magnificent performance the ministers told him that as Paramjyoti was the servant of the Three-eyed Lord, nobody could defeat him. Hearing that he was a devotee, the king became scared, of having sent a devotee to the killing battlefield. The king gave him lots of gifts and properties and requested him to serve the Lord, dedicating his time for that.

Paranjyoti returned to his town and spent his time in serving the Lord in Ganapathichram temple of the town. He got married to a girl called Venkattutuna Nangai who was also devoted to Shiva.

Siruthondar (Paranjyoti), used to feed the devotees and then only partake his food. He followed this ritual regularly.

His hospitality and devotion was known in every nook and corner of the kingdom. He was fondly called Siruthondar (small servant). The couple got a son and named him Chirala Dhevar. Siruthondar and his wife celebrated the birth of the child in a very grand manner. He generously donated to devotees and followed all rituals, including reciting of Vedas by pundits. The boy was brought up with utmost care by his parents. When he was three, they sent him to school to learn various arts.

One day Thiru Gnana Samabandar came there. Siruthondar held his soft feet on his head and saluted him. The saint stayed with him and praised his devotion to God and sang a hymn there.

The Lord wanted to demonstrate that great devotees are capable of doing deeds which are terrible to think of, for others. He assumed the form of Bhairagi.

The God who feeds the entire world, acting as if he was terribly hungry came to the devotee's house. Only his wife was there. He asked for the servant of the Lord in the house, who every day fed the devotees. Realizing that a sage had come, Nangai came out and saluting him, said that her husband had gone out. She invited him to come inside. The Lord replied that he would not come inside the house where a woman was alone. The lady told Him that as her husband did not find a single devotee that day, had gone searching for one. She said that he would be very happy if he knew that a devotee had come on his own. She asked him to sit inside the house. But he would not enter the house without the devotee being present, and stood waiting for him under a tree, near the temple.

Siruthondar came back sadly unable to find any devotee. His wife told him that a devotee from the north, in the form of Bhairagi, had come and was waiting near the temple tree. Siruthondar went to the Lord and saluted him. The Lord asked him, "Are you the great small servant?"

Nayanar replied that he was not worthy of any praise, but out of mercy the devotees call him so. The sage said that he was from the north and the food he wanted would be difficult to prepare. He wanted a life to be cooked, that took a human in the age not exceeding five, having no physical impairments, the only child in the family and the child's parents should cook it happily!

The devotee told his wife the type of food the sage asked for. They decided to cook their loving young son for the devotee. The father went and brought the child from school. He bathed him, cleaned his body completely. With the mother holding the child's hands and legs, and the child enjoying this great deed, the father cut his head. Removing the head, considering it would not be good for a feast; the loving mother cooked the rest of the body with other food materials. Then, Siruthondar invited the sage to eat, begging pardon for the delay in preparing the feast. Nangai served the rice, meat and all the food materials in a plate over a white cloth. The sage asked them whether they cooked all the parts of the child. They replied in the affirmative, but said that as the head would not be good, did not cook it. The Lord said that he liked that also. Nangai then cooked the head too, and gave that part too.

Now the Lord ordered him to bring another devotee to eat with Him. Siruthondar searched but came back unable to find one. The Lord said that as Siruthondar himself was a good devotee, he should eat with him. When Siruthondar was about to eat, the Lord stopped him asking him what was the hurry, while he Himself, who ate once in six months, had not started. The Lord then asked him to call his son. Siruthondar was shocked and speechless. The sage refused to eat without his son being present. The couple then went outside and called out for their son, loudly. "Oh! My dear child, Chirala! Come fast to make the devotee have his feast. Their son came running as if he was returning from school!

The couple embraced and kissed him thinking they could now be blessed by the devotee accepting their feast. When they came inside the house they were shocked at the absence of the Bhairagi as well as the meat that was cooked.

The Lord appeared before them with Parvathi and his young, beautiful son Muruga on the Holy Bull. Blessing the devotee, his beloved wife and loving son the Lord, took them with him.

Ever since the ascension of Siruthondar Nayanaar, a festival known as 'Amutu Padai' is being celebrated in Tirucchengkaattangudi. Two days are set apart (Chittirai-Barani and Aippasi-Barani) as the Vratha, fulfillment days, by the Shivagaamas as the Bhairava visiting Siruthondar, said: "We eat, but once in six months." It is on a Chittirai-Barani, that Nayanaar gained ascension.

Tirucchengkaattangudi

52

SOMASI MARA NAYANAR

Somasi Mara Nayanar was a Brahmin priest. He was born in Thiruvambar (Ambal) in Nagapatinam district. He was an ardent devotee of Lord Shiva and was an intense practitioner of Somayajans (sacrifices).He served all the Shiva devotees immaterial of their caste. He was also against rigid caste rules that were then prevalent. He also firmly believed in reciting the Pancharkshar mantra of Shiva. Shiva Panchkshara stostra is written in praise of Lord Shiva. The sloka describes the appearance and qualities of the lord as well as the worship of Shiva.

Aum namah shivaya, shivaya namah aum
Aum namah shivaya, shivaya namah aum

Legend

Sri Mahakalanathar Temple dedicated to lord was located in Thirumankalam. Somasi Nayanar and his wife Susheela were living in the town.Somasi wanted to perform a soma – yajna in honour of the Lord. He also desired that Lard Shiva appear in person to accept the offerings. He approached Sundarar who was ill and requested him to pray to Lord to be present during the yajna. He also kept sending thoovali – a native herb to cure cough and fever. At Sundarar's entreaty, Lord Shiva promised to attend the yajna. The news that Lord Shiva would attend the yagna spread like wildfire. Many saints, scholars, sages, devotees and common folk gathered on that day to see the yajna and Lord Shiva. At the appointed auspicious hour, Shiva arrived with his wife Parvathi and sons Ganesha and Karthikeya in the disguise of a tribal family. He was accompanied by four Vedas as dogs and dead calf. The presence of this family shocked the crowd and also Nayanar who was performing the yajna. Seeing the reaction and worry of those present, Ganesha assumed his true form and exposed the true identity of all. Overwhelmed with joy and devotion, Naynarar offered him the havir. Shiva appeared with Parvathi in his true form and blessed the Nayanar and all those who gathered there to worship him.

Sri Mahakalanthar Temple

Somasira Nayanar
Illustration courtesy: Ramalingar Paini Mandram

53

SUNDARAMURTHY NAYANAR

Thou art half woman. Thyself
Ganga is in thy long hair,
Full well canst thou comprehend
Burden of woman so fair

–Sundarar

Sundaramurthy was a prominent Nayanar. He was a poet –saint. He was born in Thirunavalur village in Thirumunaippadi Nadu (Cuddlore dist) Tamil Nadu. He was born to Sadya Nayanar and Iasaiganiyar.Both the parents are Shiva devotees and Nayanars. Sundarar was fondly called as "Thambiram" (comrade of lord Shiva) and Vanthodan. He was a contemporary of Chola King Cheraman Perumal and Kotpuli Nayanar.

There is a legend associated with Sundara's life. He was once an attendant of Lord Shiva in Mount Kailas. He went by name Aalala Sundaran. While serving the Lord, he saw two beautiful girls –Aninthithai and Kamalini who were attendants to Goddess Parvathi. He wanted to marry them. Lord Shiva blessed them to be born on earth.

Alala Sundaran was born as Nambiyurar, Kamalini as Paravai Nachiyar and Aninthithai as Sangili Nachiyar in different locations.

Thiruvanai Nallur temple

When Sundarar's wedding was about to take place, Lord Shiva appeared and stopped the marriage. Shiva visited the wedding venue in the guise of an old ascetic. He declared that Sundarar was meant to be his servant and had proof that his grandfather had pledged him as his servant on a palm leaf manuscript. The invitees to the marriage ridiculed and made fun of him and called him madman (Pithan). They also demanded that they see the palm leaf agreement. When the palm leaf was shown, the Vedic scholars concluded that the contract was genuine and Sundarar has to oblige the old man. Sundarar followed the old man to Thiruvennainalur village and then to Thiiruvararutturai Shiva temple. The old man told Sundarar that the document was only for name sake and he wanted Sundarar to recollect that he was actually Alalarsundarar, a servitor of the Lord in Kailas. Lord also told him, he will be called "Vanthodan" (the argumentative devotee) and advised him to sing in Tamil and move around to many Shiva temples in Tamil Nadu. Sundarar pursued the promise to Lord and hopped from one temple to another. He came to Thiruvarur where he fell in love with a girl named Paravayar of Rudra Kanyakayar caste of female ascetics.

One another nayanmar Kotipuliyar was immensely pleased by the services of Sundarar and offered Sundarar hand of his daughter. But Sundarar declined and instantly picked up the girl and put her in his lap and dedicated a hymn to Shiva. He concluded the hymn saying that the girl was equivalent to his daughter.

In Thiruvattriyur, near Chennai he prayed at the Thiyagaraja temple where he saw a farmer's girl, Sangiliyar who was making flower garments. He married her and promised never to leave her.

Tirupunkoor temple

At Tirupunkoor near Chidambaram, a local Chola prince requested Sundarar to help him in solving a major problem. The region had no rain for a very long time and requested Sundarar to save the region from calamity. The prince also offered 12 acres of land to the temple if rains come by the efforts of Sundarar. Sundarar sang a pathigam and rains lashed the area. The region faced a similar problem of draught after many years. Sundarar was summoned by the prince once again and he sang and soon there was a very heavy downpour. The prince happily gave another 12 acres to the temple.

Avanashi Temple

At Avanashi(near Coimbatore) Sundarar performed a miracle by getting back to life an eight year old boy who had died many years ago. On hearing his hymn Lord Shiva was moved and gave life to the boy who was swallowed by a crocodile. The boy came out of the mouth of the same crocodile alive.

Thiruvarur temple

In, Thiruvarur Sundarar recited Thirutondar Thokai. Here he refers to himself as the servant of servants of the Saivite saints. His fame reached the ears of Cheraman Perumal who came to see him at Thiruvarur. Both of them embarked on a pilgrimage. Sundarar was tired of life and was taken to heaven by a white elephant.

54

THIRU GNANA SAMBANDAR

Srivapada Hridyar of Sirkazhi had no children. He prayed to Lord Shiva for the boon of a son who would spread the greatness of Shiva. The Lord responded to his prayer and soon his wife gave birth to a beautiful divine child. Sambandar was born.

When Sambandar was three years old, his father took him to the nearby Shiva temple. He left the child on the steps of the tank and went to take a dip in the tank. The child suddenly started crying in hunger. Seeing the child crying, Goddess Parvathi descended from heaven and fed the child. After taking his bath, his father came to take the child and was shocked to see a golden cup in the child's hand. (The golden cup in which goddess Parvati gave him milk). The father asked the child who had fed him; the child pointed to the sky and then responded with a hymn "Thodudaya Seviyan."

At the age of six, the young child began to express his spiritual dimensions, singing hymns in praise of the Lord. Soon he started gaining hundreds of followers who dedicatedly accompanied him to Shiva temples. Sambandar went on a long voyage to many Shiva temples. On one occasion, he met Thiru Nilakanda Yazhpanar who was renowned for playing the stringed instrument –Yazh. Sambandar was very pleased to hear the Nayanar play the instrument and acceded to his request to accompany him to temples.

Both Sambandar and Yazhpanar visited Lord Nataraja temple at Chidambaram. A big crowd of devotees were waiting for them at the Southern entrance of the temple.

Thillai Anthanars were also waiting to receive them, singing Vedic hymns. Sambandar was stunned to see the beauty of Lord Nataraja and Goddess Sivakami. Sambandar also prostrated before the Ganas (Arthanars).

He is said to have sung over 16,000 pathigams. Only 383 could be retrieved.

Miracle performed

In Mylapore (ChennaI), there lived a merchant by name Sivanesar. He was a staunch devotee of Lord Shiva. He was very wealthy but had no children. In answer to his sincere prayer for a child, Lord Shiva blessed him with a female child. The child was born and the couple named her as Poompavai. Sivanesar heard about Sambandar and thought that he would be an ideal match for his daughter.

One day, when Poompavai was gathering flowers in the garden, a snake bit her and she died immediately. Despite the best efforts, he could not bring her back to life. He cremated the body of his daughter and collected the ash. He kept the ash in an earthen pot. Daily he used to decorate the pot with flowers and meditate on Sambandar.

At that time Sambandar came to Thiruvotriyur. The news of Sambandar's arrival reached Sivanesar. Sivanesar erected a big pandal from Mylapore to Thiruvotriyur to welcome Sambandar. Sambandar was aware of the tragedy that fell on Sivanesar and also his worship of the pot with ashes of his daughter.

Sundarar wanted to please the Shiva devotee by brining his daughter to life. He came to Mylapore and after singing hymns on Shiva asked Sivanesar to bring the pot with ash. Sambandar sang a hymn- Oh ! Poompavai, the very purpose of human birth in this world is to serve the Lord and his devotees, and feast the eyes by seeing the festivals of Lord Shiva. If this is true, arise in the presence of all. Are you going away without seeing the festival? When he was half way through another series of hymns, Poompavai emerged from the pot as a beautiful 12 year old girl. Sivanesar and Poompavai fell at the feet of Sambandar.Sivanesar entreated Sambandar to accept the girl as his wife. Sambandar, however explained that the young Poompavai whom Sivanesar mentally offered to him was dead. The present rebirth of Poomapavai was like his daughter.Sivanesaar accepted the advice of Sundarar. He built an ashrama for his daughter where she spent the rest of her life in worship of Lord.Shiva.

Sambandar returned to Sirkazhi at the age of 16. His father wanted him to get married but he expressed his desire to be engaged in worshipping Lord Shiva. But his father persisted and got him engaged to the daughter of Nambi andar Nambi. The wedding was to take place at Nallur Perumanam. Sambandar went to the temple, worshipped Lord Shiva and got his blessings.

Sambandar in his wedding dress took his seat on a pearl palanquin, the local devotees and villagers sang “Long live Sambandar”. At the venue of the wedding, Sambandar held his wife’s hand and went around the sacred fire. Thereafter, the young couple went to the temple accompanied by a large number of devotees. Sambandar sang a pathigam pleading for his liberation. The Lord responded saying "Oh! Sambandar, you, your wife and all the devotees who are with you at the wedding will merge in the Shiva Jothi and come to my abode".

A huge red effulgent light appeared from heaven. Sambandar and the entire gathering of devotees merged in the light of Shiva.

Sirkazhi temple

Chidambaram Temple: Mahapriayava.com

55

THIRU KURIPPUI THODA NAYANAR

This is the sunset hour when the Lord Shiva,
Mahadev, Lord of Destruction, Ghosts and Spirits,
Riding the divine Nanda, His favorite bull,
Goes through the World of men to observe
And with His Three Eyes sees the souls of men.
I worship the Lord in His form as the Shiva Lingam,
Symbol of His creative energy and regeneration.
There is none like Him, higher or greater
In all the three worlds of His creation........Dadaji

Kanchipuram in Tamil Nadu is famous for its various temples. Puranas say that among the towns, it is the best. It was the capital of the Pallavas. It is said that one who is born in Kanchipuram attains mukti. Tamil poets praise Kanchipuram in their works. All the three Thevaram saints have visited Kanchi and sang hymns.Sekkizhar who hails from Kanchi has sung its glories in 110 verses while narrating the story of Thirukurippu Thondar Nayanar. When Uma playfully held her hands and closed Shiva's eyes, the world stopped functioning. For this peccadillo, Uma wanted to perform tapas and dhana in Kanchipuram, as per advice of Shiva. She went there, stood on a needle's end and performed severe penance, in front of a fire. She was eating only dry leaves. She made a linga from the river sand and performed pujas. When flash floods came in Kamba river and the sand Linga was about to be dissolved, she embraced the Shivalinga with her breasts and hands. Even today, in Kanchi Ekambaranatha Swami temple, the Shiva linga made of sand is having the niche of breasts and bangles! Since the Shiva Lingam is made of sand, there is no ablution with water and milk. There is only application of punugu, sandal, camphor and kasturi.

Arunagiri Nathar says that she performed 32 types of dhana, right from feeding the poor and hungry, conducting marriage of young girls, giving medicine for the sick, giving clothes for the needy, feeding animals, running patasalas for children, sponsoring Vedic sacrifices etc., After tapas and dhana, she was asked by Shiva to come to Arunachala for reunion with Him. When Ravana attempted to pull Kailash and was punished by Shiva in Kailas, he was asked to go to Kanchipuram and pay his retribution.

Thirukurippu Thondar, is one of the 63 Saivite Saints. He was a washerman and lived in Kanchipuram. His name is derived from, 'the one who understands the devotees' minds and does service. He would volunteer to wash devotee's cloths, without being asked. This understanding earned him the name Thirukurippu Thondar. He used to constantly utter the name of Shiva as he washed and felt that his work washed away the sins of his previous births.

Once God decided to test his true devotion. Shiva took the form of an old man wearing only dirty clothes. On seeing the old man, Nayanar welcomed him and agreed to wash his clothes. The old man gave his consent on one condition. He was using the cloths to protect himself from cold and therefore they should be returned by evening as he would be leaving town.

Tirukurippu Thondar readily agreed and went to the river bank. He managed to wash the clothes well after several attempts. By the time, it was evening and rain started. Nayanar was upset as rain poured non- stop till the night. Feeling sad and restless, he prayed to Lord Shiva. Nayanar also offered new cloth pieces from home. Shiva in disguise refused. Nayanar decided to punish himself for the failure. He went to hit his head on the washing stone and die. As he did so, the stone turned soft and the Divine hand held his head.

Shiva then appeared with Uma Devi and took him to heaven. His sincerity had been revealed to the world.

56

THIRUMULA NAYANAR

Surrender your desire, even unto the Lord
The more you desire, the more sorrows,
The more you give up,
The more your bliss shall be
Thirumandiram

Thirumoolar was known as "Sundaranatha". He was one of the greatest mystics of India. He was a saint, traditionally allotted a date of 3000 BC and presumed to have lived for 3000 years. He was one of the 18 Siddhas. His main contribution is 'Thirumandhiram' that describes various aspects of science, medicine, human beings and life. As a student, he studied with Guru Agasthiar in Pothigai region.

Agasthiar was a Siddha, Saint and Rishi. His works are very vast in the field of medicine, Sithandham, Vedhantham, Philosophy and Tamil literature. Those days education meant 'gurukulavasam'. When Thirumoolar completed his studies in Tamil, guru Agasthiar, sponsored him to "Nandeeswaran" for pursuing further studies in Sanskrit language about Veda Agamam.

After completion of his tutelage under Nandeeswarar at Mount Kailas, Thirumoolar came down to meet his Guru Agasthiyar who lived in Podhigai region in Tamil Nadu. He came to Avaduthurai to have a darshan of the Lord and sang in praise of the Lord's love for pasus (cows) there. He continued his journey towards Podhigai. Suddenly, he saw cows crying on the river bank. Mulan, a herdsman of village Sattanur, died when he brought the cows for grazing on the banks of the river. The cows went around the body licking and crying. Realizing that if Mulan came back alive, the cows would get consoled, Sundaranatha, a splendid Siddha fortified his body and introduced his soul into the body of the herdsman, through the air. He rose as Thirumular. The cows, relieved of their gloom, went around happily, grazing on the riverbanks. The cows, then thinking of their calves, started walking back towards the village. The sage followed them to Sattanur.

Wife of Mular saw him delay while entering the house. She rushed to touch him, but he resisted. He informed her of what had happened. Then, he moved to a monastery and went into meditation. The wife of Mular was upset and convinced the wise men of the village that he was either ill or possessed. Soon they realized that the shepherd was dead and that a sage had entered his body. Mular returned to Thiruavaduthurai and sat under the BO tree, west of the temple walls, in subconscious trance. Under the shade of the Bo-tree, Thirumoolar sang the holy "Thirumandiram" which consists of over 3,000 verses. These verses were sung by him spontaneously, every now and then, when he regained consciousness from his trance.

Thirumandiram is the tenth thirumurai in the Tamil saivaite 'Panniru Thirumurai'.

"Nan petra inbam peruga ivvaiyagam
Wan patri nindra marai porul sollidien
Voon patri nindra vunarvuru Mandhiram
Than patra patra thalai padum thane"

Thirumoolar observed that the pleasure of acquiring Asthamasiddhi as enjoyed by him was available to all in the world. There are no restrictions.

In his thought provoking Thirumandiram, Thirumular says that the omnipotent cannot be transcribed in a single place nor measured, nor has any names but can only to be experienced:

Thirumoolar even wrote in Thirumandiram about the various stages of development of a baby in its mother's womb. He is said to have absorbed the teachings of "Shri Patanjali Maharishi".

Tirumoolar is also considered as the founder of the "Tamil Siddha" system. He describes the ways and means of attaining an immortal body, called "Kayasiddhi". Unlike the homogeneous and heterogeneous systems of Indian philosophy which emphasized the ephemerality of the physical body, the Siddha system of Tirumoolar advocated a fresh theory of preserving the body so that the soul would continue its existence (Udambai valarthen uyir valarthenae).

Thirumoolar teaches the ethics of Ahimsa, abstinence from slaughtering, meat- eating and drinking. He condemns coveting another man's wife. Like the crow inviting its group to partake the food, people should be liberal in exercising charity, without any discrimination. Thirumular has stated unequivocally in his Thirumandiram "one caste and one God only".

Mount Kailas

Thirumular
Illustration courtesy: Ramalingar Paini Mandram

57

THIRUNALAIPOVAR NAYANAR (NANDANAR)

In the paddy fields, Nandanar sat in a daze,
Soaking in the sun, the cattle grazed.
In the swaying husks of the golden field,
Images of Lord Shiva, he did see.
In every grain, His eyes did shine,
Dancing, smiling, His face divine...
Hema from Zurich......

Adanur on the bank of river Kolladam was a fertile village with vast green fields and fragrant groves. A slum stood amidst such splendour. The poorest section of the village crushed and thrashed grain for a living. They worked hard all day and spent the evenings beating drums and singing. Nandanar was born here. He belonged to the untouchable (paraiya) caste. He lost his father at a very early age. He grew up hearing stories of Shiva and his miraculous deeds. He fell in paternal love for Shiva. He used to sing his glories daily, composing songs. Nandanar made drums and parts of instruments like Veena and Yaazhi that are played to worship God. He offered leather and straps for drums and strings for harps and violin. He also served as a village servant, watchman and labourer as well as the "town crier" who used to beat the drums.

During his times, Dalits were not allowed to enter temples. So, Nandanar faithfully used to stand outside the Shiva temple and sing hymns on the Lord. He harboured a strong urge to pay his respects to Shiva at Shivalokanathar temple, Thiruppunkoor. He stood outside the temple, but the huge stone Nandi (mount of Shiva) blocked his path of vision of the God. Nandi is seen in all Shiva temples facing the idol of Shiva. Seeing the plight of His devotee, Shiva ordered Nandi to move a little to enable Nandanar to have darshan. Nandi moved and Nandanar had full view of Shiva. The Dwara palakas were wonder struck by this order of the Lord and opened their mouth wide which is seen in the temple even today.

In joy, Nandanar hastily cleaned up the surroundings of the temple and dug a pond in honour of Shiva. The temple tank was dug in a day with the help of Lord Ganesha, according to legend. He then returned to Adanur.

Nandanar had taken a day off to visit the temple and his landlord was unhappy with him. However, Nandanar promised to put in extra effort and compensate. Nandanar was also very keen to visit Chidambaram. He heard so much about Nataraja and His cosmic dance. He heard about Arudhra Darshan and told everyone in his anxiety, that he would visit Chidambaram, the very next day. But he never went out of the village. So the villagers called him Thirunalipovar (He will go tomorrow).

One day, Nandanar approached his landlord for a day off to go to Chidambaram. After pleading and begging, the landlord agreed to grant him leave on one condition- that he could go after harvesting the 250 acres of land. Knowing that the landlord was deliberately putting him in a fix, he cried the whole night appealing to God for help. The next day, he was surprised to see the entire field harvested. The landlord saw the miracle and fell at the feet of Nandanar. He gave him money to go to Chidambaram.

Nandanar with devotion and joy reached the outskirts of Chidambaram. He was scared to set foot in the town as he belonged to the untouchable class. From a distance, he saw the smoke of fire sacrifices and also heard the Vedic chants. Contemplating how to see Nataraja, he fell asleep. Shiva appeared in his dream and told him to enter the temple through a holy fire. Shiva then ordained the priests in the temple to prepare a pyre. Nandanar entered the sacred fire chanting "Om namashivaya" and reappeared in a purified form. He looked like a Brahmin saint wearing the sacred thread and body smeared with holy ash. The devas showered flowers from Heaven and Nayanar entered the garbhagraha and embraced the icon of Nataraja and disappeared to be with Shiva.

Nandanar's story is mentioned in the Sthala purana of Chidambaram. He was inducted as one of the 63 saints.

Gopalakrishna Bharathi, the visionary poet of the nineteenth century has written a musical drama called 'Nandanar Charitam' which became a famous Harikatha. Bharathi added a unique divine flavor to the story of Nandanar in his opening verses.

The story of Nanda is full of joy but when telling,
It is full of the feeling of the nectar of devotion

The story of Nanda is great as it is Lord Shiva's own,
And those who hear it will lose attachments and sins.

How come, this world has an innocent one like him?
And his story is joyful to all those with two ears.

Getting dejected and later singing "Arahara",
Then dancing and saying he will reach the golden stage
(Translation by P.R.Ramachandar)

Nandanar's tale is retold in numerous ways, through folk tales, art forms like villu pattu "musical discourses", plays and literature. Few Tamil films, on Nandanar, have also been released. The 1935 film featured K.B. Sundarambal, who also performed on stage as the Nayanar, many times. The 1942 film, starring Dandapani Desikar in the lead, courted controversy for it's overly Brahmin overtones and was banned in Kolar Gold fields after protests by Dalits. The ban was lifted after Desikar apologized to the Dalits for being part of the climax, which featured the fire-purification. Another film on Nandanar was released in 1943.

N.S. Krishnan presented the story as a "narrative art form. Even today, the story of Nandanar is very popular among Indians throughout the world.

River Kolladam

58

THIRU NEELAKANTA NAYANAR

Thiru Neelankanta Nayanar lived in the holy town Chidambaram. He was a dedicated devotee of Lord Shiva and always ready to serve devotees of Shiva. He was a potter by profession and caste. He had a pious and dutiful wife and lived happily. He also made beautiful begging bowls of clay and offered to devotees free. He kept talking about Lord Shiva all the time and how he consumed poison.

Thiru Neelakanta Nayanar forgetting about god and home once succumbed to passion. He visited a house of a prostitute. When he returned home, his faithful and pious wife was able to understand about his visit to a harlot's house. Though she despised his action, she continued to do her duty towards the husband. She decided not to have sexual relation with him. Nayanar was unable to understand his wife's behavior. One day, he tried to get intimate with her; she turned him back saying "in the name of Neelakanta, I ask you, do not touch us." She inadvertently said "us" as she took the name of the Lord.

Neelakanta Nayanar promised that he would never touch any woman in the world. But the couple continued to live without anyone knowing what happened between them. Both grew old.

At that stage, Lord Shiva wanted to expose their true devotion and immortalize them.

Lord took the disguise of a Shiva Yogi and visited Nayanar's home. Neelakanatar welcomed him and showered on him best of hospitality. The Yogi then made a request to keep his begging bowl safely till he returned after a few days. The yogi also explained that the begging bowl was rare with a power of purifying anything that comes in contact with it. Neelakantar's kept the bowl safely in his house.

After a long time, Shiva made the bowl disappear from home. Then he came back to Neelakantar's home and demanded that the bowl be returned to him. At that juncture, Neelakantar realized that the bowl was missing. He frantically searched every nook and corner of his house but could not locate the bowl. He immediately asked the yogi to pardon him. The yogi called him a thief lier and a cheat. Neelakantar offered to give the yogi, a better and costlier one. Yogi categorically refused. He pleaded with the yogi that he was innocent. The yogi then asked Neelakantar to hold his wife's hand and swear if he was not guilty. The matter went to court. The court upheld Shiva yogi's request.

Neelakantar got into the tank, along with his wife; they had a stick in their hand each holding, one end of it. Yogi objected to it and said that Neelakantar should actually hold his wife's hand with his own. Unable to concede to the order, Neelakantar narrated what happened and why he could not hold his wife's hand owing to his folly. Neelakantar and his wife caught hold of the two ends of the stick and took a dip in the tank. At that moment, a miracle happened. As they emerged from the water, they both shone like a young couple. The Shiva yogi disappeared. Lord Shiva and Parvathy appeared in the sky and blessed all those who had assembled.

59

THIRU NILAKANTA YAZHPANAR

The life of Thiru Nilakanta Yazpanar is described in the Tamil Periya Puranam by Sekkizhar in 12th century.

Thiru Nilakanta Yazhpanar was born in Erukattanpulliyur in the Chola Kingdom. He belonged to the Tami Panar community. Panars are basically wandering musicians. Yazh panar denotes that the occupation of panar is to play the yazh. Yazh panar was a staunch devotee of Lord Shiva. He had developed extraordinary skill in playing the musical instrument and attracted people. Yazh panar being a devotee of Lord Shiva travelled to many Shiva temples and played hymns on Lord. Since Yazh panar belonged to a low caste, he was not allowed to enter the temples. Yet with a will to please God, he stood at the entrance of temples and played yazh.

One day, he reached Madurai which was under the rule of Pandyas. He stood at the entrance of Thiruaalvai Temple and played the yazh. The temple is one of the 275 Thevara Shiva sthalam. It is located at the heart of Madurai. The melodies divine music sailed through the temple and Lord was pleased. Lord Shiva appeared in the dream of the priests and asked them to escort Yazhpanar to the sanctum sanctorium. A heavenly voice suggested that Nayanar be given a golden seat so that his yazh was not placed on the wet floor of the temple. Nayanar stood on the golden seat and sang the glory of Shiva.

Then, Yazhpanar went to Thyagaraja Tempe at Thiruvarur. He played the yazh outside the temple as usual. The Lord of the temple invited him to come in through the northern entrance which the god opened for him. Yazhpanar sang in praise of lord there.

Yazhpanar pursued his pilgrimage to many Shiva temples. He met Sambandar at the Sattinathar Temple at Sirkali. Yazhpanar accompanied Sambandar in his travel. Sambandar composed many songs on Lord Shiva and Yazhpanar played music for the songs. Both went to Chidambaram and continued to visit many Shiva temples.

After sometime, Yazhpanar attended the wedding of Sambandar in Achalapuram. Thiruneelanakka Nayanar conducted the rituals. After the wedding ceremony, all the guests and the newlywed went to Thirumananallur. Lord Shiva appeared as "jothi" and blessed all the attendees of the wedding including Nilakanta Yazhpanar to heavenly abode. Stunned by the sight of jothi, in ecstasy he sang his last pathigam expressing the greatness and divine drawing power of Na Ma Shivaya".

It is interesting to note that Nilakanta Yazhpanar was the first to set music to the songs of a Nayanar. He set a "precedent for musical performance of the Thevaram hymns" which later encouraged Tevaram recitals in temples and concerts. Thivaram in musical format enhanced its charm as many Thivaram musical classes sprung up all over Tamil Nadui and overseas. It is also said that the music of Thevaram was lost. Nambiyandar Nambi visited Thiru Nilakanta Yazhpanars hometown to recover it. A Panar woman is said to have revealed to him that she got to know by a "divine revelation".

Neelakanda Yaazhpana Nayanar: the Sakoda Yaazh - the musical instrument depicted here was lost in time.

60

THIRUNAVUKKARASAR- APPAR

Thirunavukkarasar means 'King of the tongue'. Thirunavukkarasar (Appar) was born at Thiruvamur, in Thirumunaipadinadu, on the banks of the river Pennai. It was here that both Thirunvakakarasar and Sundarar were born. He was born in a Velan family to Puhalanar and Madiniyar. The couple had a daughter first, named Thilakavati. A few years later they had a son Marulnikkiyar (remover of illusion). The boy grew up in typical local conventions and started learning in the traditional way. When Thilakavathi was twelve, the local army chief Kaliappakaiyar wanted to marry her. Before the marriage could be conducted, war broke out with the king of the North. Kaliappakaiyar went to the war front and died in the battlefield. Meanwhile Thilakavati's parents also died.

Grief stricken, Thilakavati prepared to commit immolation. Marulnikkiyar appealed to her not to do so for his sake. Thilakavati then took to a life of penance. Marulnikkiyar turned a Jain and joined a monastery. He was given the name of Dharmasena. Thilakavati took to the Saivite path and lived in Thiruvadigai. She spent her life cleaning the temple premises, and making flower garlands for worship. However the thought that her brother had become a Jain tormented her. She prayed to Lord Shiva to make him a Shiva devotee. Shiva appeared in her dream and blessed her.

While in the monastery, Dharmasena suffered from unbearable stomach pain. The Jains proclaimed that his disease was incurable. He sent word to his sister about his ailment. She told the messenger that she would not enter the Jain monastery to see her brother. Dharmasena left the monastery and came to the mutt where Thilakavatiyar stayed. He requested her to cure him. She suggested that he devote himself to Lord Shiva.

Next morning, both sister and brother went to the temple of Virattana at Thiruvadigai. Thilakavati chanted the Pancakshara mantra and gave the sacred ashes to her brother. Wearing the ashes, he prostrated before Shiva and sung the hymn 'kurrayinavaru vilakku'.

Thou takest not my deadly pain away,
My torments, Nandi rider, never cease;
At thy feet would I worship night and day?
But since my bowels writhe, and ne'er find peace
I can no more! O! Sire, to thee I cry
Who dwell'st by Kedila, in Athihai....

The stomach ache vanished. A divine voice was heard calling him Navukkarasu. The Jains felt that Dharmasena's desertion was a great blow to their religion. They thought that if the King came to know about this incident, he too would embrace Saivism. They informed the Pallava ruler, who was a Jain about Dharmasena's desertion. The enraged, king ordered the death of Thirunavukkarasu.

The king sent his messengers to fetch Navukkarasar from Thiruvadigai. The saint refused to accompany them, stating that he would not fear death. The king ordered that he be confined in a lime kiln. After seven days, when the kiln was opened the saint emerged unhurt.

Navukkarasar was then administered a poison which again did him no harm. As a third step, the king, let loose the royal elephant against him. The ferocious elephant fell at his feet.

In yet another attempt to kill the saint, he was ordered to be tied to a slab of stone and thrown into the sea. While tied to a heavy stone, he sang another hymn, invoking the sacred power of Namasshivaya. The stone slab started floating like a wooden plank and carried him to Thiruppadhiripuliyur (Cudddalore).

The king by now realized the truth, repented for his sins, denounced the Jains and surrendered to the sage. The king built a temple for the Lord called Gunaparavichcharam.

Thirunavukkarasar then visited many Shiva shetras including Thiruvennainallur, Amattur, Thirukkoyilur and Pennagadam. He reached Chidambaram and entered the temple through its western gate. In ten verses, he exclaimed "My Lord I have come here to behold your cosmic dance". It was here that Thirunavukarasa heard about Gnanasambandar and went to meet him at Sirkali. On seeing Sambandar, Thirunavukkarasar, fell at his feet. Sambandar in return fell at the feet of Navukkarasar, and respectfully addressed him as "Appar" (Father).

Appar then proceeded to Tingalur to meet Saint Appudi Adigal. Appudi was his great admirer. In his village, Appudi had established, a feeding house, a well, a tank, and a watershed, all named after Appar. When Appar came to the village, he was surprised to see his name everywhere. Appar continued his pilgrimage and reached Thiruvarur, where he met saint Nambiandi, another great Saivaite.

Once when Appar was residing at Thiruviralimalai in the company of Sambandar, the country faced a severe drought. Lord came to their rescue and gifted a gold coin daily, one for Appar and one for Sambandar. The coin used to appear on the balipitha in the east and west of the temple. With that coin, both the Saints fed thousands of devotees.

Appar went to Kanchipuram to visit Ekambaram, Mayanam, Merrali and other Shiva temples. From Kanchi, he went to Thiruvorriyur, visiting en route Thirukalukunram, Thiruvanmiyur and Mylapore. He then proceeded to Thiruvalangadu, Karaikal and Kalahasti. From Kalahasti, he continued the journey and reached Varanasi. Having worshipped Shiva at Varanasi, he reached "Karcuram´.After reaching a certain height Appar could not climb any further. At that place, a Saivaite saint appeared and Appar told him that he was going to the summit of Kailas. The saint advised Appar to turn back as Kailas was beyond the reach of even Devas. Appar replied that he would not return with his body, without beholding Lord Shiva on Kailas. Thereupon, the sage, who was none other than Shiva in disguise, appeared before Appar and blessed him.

Appar, later visited Madurai temple and met the Pandya king Nedumaran and queen Mangaiyarkarasi. From there he went to Thiruppuvanam and Rameswaram. On a Sadaya in the month of Chittrai, he sang the hymn "Lord, I am reaching your sacred feet" and passed away.

Pasupatheeswarar Temple, Thiruvamur

61

THIRU NEELANAKKA NAYANAR

Thiruneelanakka also known as Nilanakkar was born in Sattamangai (Thirusanthamanai), a town in Chola Kingdom. The town is now known as Seethamangai in Tamil Nadu. The Ayavanheewarar temple of Lord Shiva is located here.

Thiruneelanakka belonged to the Brahmin community whose duty was to recite Vedas. He was an expert in Vedas and an ardent devotee of Lord Shiva. He served Shiva devotees by washing their feet and entertaining them at home. He regularly worshipped in the Shiva temple as per the Agamic texts. Agamas mean tradition that has come down.

Once, on a full moon day (Poornima) Thiruneelanakka Nayanar and his wife went to the Shiva temple. While Nayanar was performing his daily ritual worship, a spider fell on the Shiva Lingam. Nayanar's wife instinctively blew away the spider. While blowing away the spider, some saliva could have fallen on the Lingam. Nayanar considered this act as sacrilegious. His wife however told him that she blew away the spider as per traditional practice only. Turning angry, Nayanar said that she had contaminated the Lingam with her saliva. He further told her that she should have removed the spider by some other way. Nayanar abandoned his wife and apologized to God.

Nayanar's wife spent the night in the temple. Nayanar went home and slept. Lord Shiva appeared in Nayanar's dream. His whole body, except for a small part was swollen due to the spider's poison. Shiva revealed to Nayanar that the normal part of the body was where his wife had spat. Immediately, Nayanar realized that true devotion means much more than rituals. Early next morning, Nayanar went dancing with joy to the temple and worshipped Ayavantheeswarar. He came back home with his wife.

At that time, Thiruneelanakka came to know that Sambandar and Thiru Nelakanta Yazhpanar were coming to his town. Nayanar decorated Sattamangai for welcoming Sambandar and his team of devotees to his home to spend the night. Sambandar suggested that Nayanar accommodate Yazhpanar and his wife in his house. Nayanar was reluctant as they belonged to the lower caste. (Even today caste discrimination exists but God considers everyone as equal).

Sundarar insisted and Nayanar reluctantly allowed them to sleep near the Homa Kunda, the fire altar that is used for sacrifices. In the middle of the night, the fire of Homa Kunda shone brilliantly giving testimony of Yazhpanar and his wife's devotion to Lord Shiva. Nayanar comprehended that devotion is superior and caste has no say. Sambandar accompanied Nayanar to the Ayavantheewarar temple and composed hymns in praise of God and his host.

After a few days, Sambandar invited Thiruneelanakka Nayanar to his wedding in Thirumananallur (Achalpuram). Nayanar officiated as the presiding priest at the wedding ceremony. After the wedding, Sambandar and his bride went to the Shivaloka Thyagar temple in Thirumananallur and appealed to Shiva for salvation. Shiva appeared as a blazing flame and granted their wish. Sambandar, his bride, wedding invitees and Thiruneelanakka Nayanar merged into the light of Shiva.

Today, the image of Thiruneelanakka Nayanar is worshipped in Ayavantheewarar temple. Nayanar is worshipped in Vaikasi (Tamil month) in his native temple.

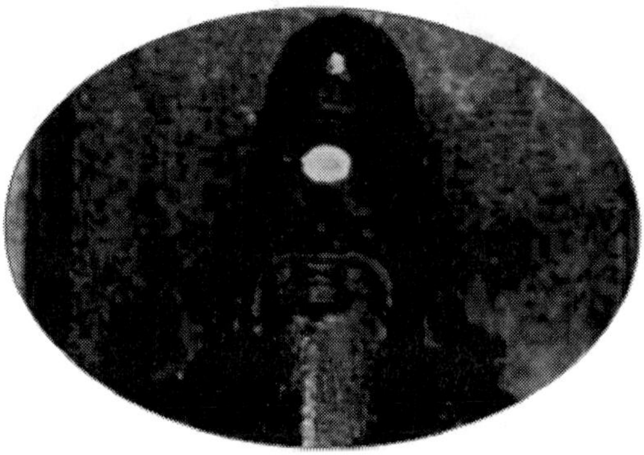

Ayavanheewarar

Ayavanheewarar temple

62

VAYILAR NAYANAR

Vayilar Nayanar hails from Mylapore, the abode of Lord Kapali and Godess Karpagambal. Vayilar was a dedicated Shiva Bhakta. He constructed temples mentally and did manasic (mental) worship. He constructed the temple of non-forgetfulness in his heart, lit the lamp of self-illumination and bathed the Lord in the waters of immortal bliss and worshipped him with abundant love. Lord Shiva seeing the devotion and spiritual love, granted him salvation.

Vayilar Nayanar's life is a lesson to devotees. Whatever may be your status in life, you can choose a divine path to worship, Shiva and attain moksha- the real goal of all.

There is a shrine for Vayilar in the Kapaleeswarar temple at Mylai.

Kapaleeswarar Temple, Mylapore

63

VIRALMINDA NAYANAR

There is this beautiful place called Shenkunrur (Thiruchchenkodu), where the God stands in the superior male-female (Ardanarishwarar) form enjoying the sandal aroma and cool breeze of the forests. The village is mostly occupied by traditional farmers.

Viralminda Nayanar was born Chenlirrur in a farmers family. He was caring much for the true devotees of Shiva. He traveled through many parts of the land and finally arrived at the town *Thiruvarur* where the Lord resides the minds of the devotees and also in the big chariot in that town. He immersed himself in that beautiful Shiva for whom the Vedas became the chariot.

In Thiruvarur there was a famous hall called *Devachiriyam,* where the great slaves of the blue throated Lord assemble and praise Shiva. Blessed are those who had the golden opportunity to see them, hear them, follow them and serve them.

Viralminda prostrated to them and stayed with them. One day Sundharar who considered himself as the slave of the slave of the slaves of Shankara, went direct to the altar of the temple without bowing to the devotees in the Divachiriyam hall. Viralmindar who noticed Sundharar proceeding without prostrating to the crowd of devotees said angrily, "That Sundharar who didn't know to pay respect to the devotees is no longer one of us. The Lord who blesses him who proceeds without saluting the slaves also is not one among us.

The Lord who accepts even the scolding of the devotees as the praises done with the best coined words enjoyed this love and angry words of Viralmindar. He gave the first line to Sundarar to sing the greatness of devotees. Sundarar composed that as the great gem *Thiru Thondakotai (a garland of ardent devotees of Lord)* which is the basic source for this *Periya puranam*. Thus, Viralmindar was instrumental in getting the excellent *Thiru Thondakotai* from Sundarar. Living long in this world which is meant for love and worship, upholding the respect of the devotees, that great devotee Viralminda stayed in a right way under the graceful feet of the Lord heading the army of the God.

Viralmindar as part of the devotees: he could excommunicate the very god of his religion and his god would consider that a great act of devotion

Sri Arthanareeswarar Temple, Thiruchengode

Sri Arthanareeswarar Temple, Thiruchengode

Arthanareeshwarar Temple is an ancient temple located in Thiruchengode, Tamil Nadu. The temple is dedicated to Arthanareeswarar (half –male, half-female of Lord Shiva.) The temple is one of the 275 shrines praised in the Thevaram hymns. The temple is considered as the 4th of the 7 Thevara Stalams in the Kongu region. Both Thirugnanasambandar and Arunagirinathar have composed hymns about the grandeur of this temple. Sambandar composed the Thiruneelakandapathipagam here to get rid of affliction of fellow travelers.

Saint Arunagirinathar has also composed Thirpugazh on Lord Muruga here. The musical wizard and composer Muthuswami Dikshitar composed "Arthanareeshwaram" in the rare raga Kumudakriya.

In the great Tamil Epic "Silapathikaram" the locale is mentioned by the name of "Neduvelkundru." It is believed that Kanagi after setting fire to Madurai called to heaven by her husband Kovalan and in anger at the peak Thiruchengode hill.

The deity of the temple is also known as Madhorubagan and Ammaiyappan. The temple was renovated many times during the reign of Chola, Pandya and Nayar Kings. A British Colonial Officer Davis also contributed to the renovation of the temple during British regime. His image can be seen in the Mukkottu Vinayar Temple.

Legends: Arthanareeswarar

It is said that Adi Kesava Perumal in the form of Vishnu appeared here and instructed Gowri on the significance of Kedara Gowri Viratam. Gowri had been performing this viratam to unite with Shiva as Arthanareeswarar.

Once, Lord Vishnu, Brahma, Indira and Sage Birungi went to Kailas to worship Lord Shiva. The vehicle of Shiva, Nandi directed them to Lord Shiva. Everyone first had the blessings of Parvathi before they had darshan of the Lord. Sage Birungi by passed Goddess Parvathi and proceeded to have the Lord's darshan. Parvathi got angry and sucked the flesh from the sage's body to stop him. Lord Shiva seeing the plight of Birungi and blessed him with a third leg. Goddess Parvathi was apologetic to the Lord for her action. After taking his pardon, Goddess Parvati along with their crew went to the hill top and performed the virtha. In return, she demanded that she should get a portion of Lord's body. The boon was granted which led to the manifestation of Arthanareeswarar. Parvathi took the left side of Shiva body.

Adiseshan

vayu

Thousands of years ago, there was a continuous fight between Adiseshan and Vayudeva as to who is mightier. Sages intervened and suggested a plan of action. Accordingly Adisesha had to press Mount Meru with his hood and Vayu had to release the pressure by his mighty strength to stop the air. But Vayu could not succeed and in a fit of anger he ceased the air in the universe. All human beings fainted. Sages and Celestials rushed to Adieseha to release his hold. Vayu hit the top of Adishesha on top of the mountain. The pieces of flesh with blood fell in three places on earth. One is Thiruvanamalai, Sri Lanka and Nagamali (Chengode).

Tiruchengode Arthanareesarar Temple

64

MANIKAVASAGAR

Manikavasagar is a Tamil poet who lived during the 9th century. He is known for his poetic work called "Thiruvasagam." Thiruvasagam is a brilliant work in Tamil literature depicting the glory and unconditional love towards Lord Shiva.Thiruvasagam is sung in most of the Saivite temples (padal petra stalangals) even today. Manikavasagar means man with words more precious than the gem stone Manikam. He was known as Thiruvaadhavoorar.

Manikavasagar was born in a village called "Thiruvadhavoor" near Madurai. His father was Sampupadhachariar and mother was Sivaganavadhiyar. He went to school at an early age and proved to be an outstanding student learing literature and art. He was pious and read religious books. He was impressed with Lord Shiva and became an ardent devotee even as a kid. As he grew up, he became prominent and drew the attention of King Arimardhana Pandiyan. He employed him as his minister and conferred the title of 'Thennavan Brahmarayan."

Significant incidents

Once King Pandyan entrusted Manikavasagar with a huge amount of money to purchase Arabian horses for his cavalry.

On his way, he met an ascetic devotee of Lord Shiva and receivced enlightenment. He realised that all material things are momentary. He forgot all about his mission and built a temple for Shiva in Thirupperunturai with the money meant for buying horses.

Thirupperunturai

The king who eagerly awaited for the arrival of the horses was getting impatient. He sent his spies in serach of Vadhavooran. The spies told the King that Vadhavooran had not gone beyond Thirupperunturai and was occupied in the construction of a temple there. Irritated and insulted, the King ordered Vadhavooran to be brought to Madurai. When Vadhavooran heard the kings order, he recollected his mission. He was aware that he had spent all the money entrusted by the king in the construction of the temple. The King's messanger came to escort him to Madurai.

Vadhavooran requested for some time and rushed to the temple. He saw an old man (Shiva in dsiguise) who advised him to go back to the king and inform him that the horses are on their way and will arrive on Avani Moolam Day.

The old man gave a diamond ring to Vadhavooran and asked him to give it as a gift from the horse trader.

On arrival at Madurai, Vadhavooran gave the ring to the king and informed him that the horses would arrive on the appointed time. A day before the arrival of the horses, there was no sign of dust or sound of horses approaching the town.

Lord Shiva wanted to have some fun. That night, all foxes from the nearby jungle got transformed into horses and arrived at dawn. The gatekeepers were stunned to see the galoping horses and a very handsome man leading the team of horse riders. The King was pleased that Vadhavooran had successfully completed his task. The leader of the team (Lord Shiva) briefed the king on how to manage the horses and the method of feeding them. The king ordered all the horses to be taken to the stable. The king wanted to ride the Arabian horse the next morning.

Lord Shiva had another plan. He transformed the horses back into foxes. The foxes started ransacking the palace and all places. They were unmanageable. The gatekeepers opened the gates and all the foxes ran away to the jungle.

The King was infuriated and inferred that Vadhavooran was practising some black magic. The King blamed Vadhavooran for this horse-fox mishap. The king gave a severe punishment to Vadhavooran. He gave orders that Vadhavooran shoud stand in the hot sand on the River bed of Vaigai. Vadhavooran stood in the burning hot sand and unable to bear the pain of burns, he pleaded to Lord Shiva. Shiva answered his prayers with heavy rain, thunder and lightning. Within a few moments, the Vaigai river was in spate. The King ordered one person from each home to rush and help in strengthening the embankment. Everyone rushed to the river side to help.

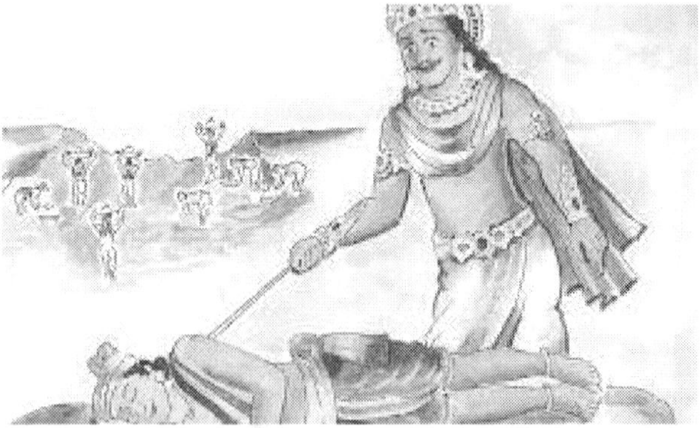

At that time, there was an old lady by name Vanthi who was living on the banks of the river. She was making "puttu" (a sweet dish made with rice andjaggery). She was a devotee of Shiva and followed the routine of offering Puttu first to the Lord and then selling them to customers. She wanted to help the King but helpless as she had none to sponsor for the job.

A hungry young man approched her and said that he was looking for a job. She said that she was also looking for someone who could carry out the King's order. The young man was ready to help but wanted payment for his labour. Vanathi said that she had no money but would give him delicious puttu in return. Overjoyed, the youngster said that his grandmother used to give him puttu and he will be too happy to work. The boy had a sumptuos delicacy of puttu in a banana leaf.

He took the spade the old lady gave him and went to the river bank where everyone was working hard to stop the flood. The boy looked around and found a big tree with spread out roots on the ground. He settled down and reclining on the bark of the tree, fell asleep.

The King happened to pass by. He was upset to see a young man sleeping while all others were working hard. He woke him up and wanted to know his whereabouts. The young man replied that he was the servant of Vanathi and went back to sleep. This attitude of the younster upset the king. He took out his whip and snapped the back of the sleeping boy.At that very instant, all the people includng the king felt the pain on their backs. The king could not understand how this had happened. He then understood that the young man was Lord Shiva. Shiva disappeared and the waters receded.

The King rushed to Vadhuvooran and begged forgivness for his hasty action. He relinquished his throne and proceeded on a pilgrimage to vaiorus Shiva kshetrams. Finally, he settled down at Chidambaram.

Sri Lanka monk visit.

The Chief of Buddist monk in the court of Sri Lanka wanted to visit Chidambaram. His mission was to establish the supremecy of Buddhist philosophy and also convert saivites to Buddhism. The Sri Lankan King and his dumb daughter accompained the monk to Chidamabaram.

On arrival in Chidambaram, the monk challenged the priests for a debate on what is superior- Hiduism or Buddhism. Manikavasagar was assigned to take on the Buddist monk in the debate as ordained by Lord Shiva in his dream.

The Buddist monk went on denigrating Saivism with abuses and lies. Stunned by the behaviour and words of the monk, Manikavasagar prayed to Goddess Saraswathi to stop this rant. At once, the flow of words from the monk's mouth stopped and he was shocked and dumbstruck.

The Sri Lankan King understood the greatness of both Hinduism and divinity of the Nayanar. He pleaded that Manikavasagar make his daughter speak. Manikavasagar appealed to Goddess Saraswathi who blessed the little girl and she started to speak. The king along with the monk got converted to Saivism. The Monk also recovered from his paralysed tongue.

Courtesy: Department of Archaeology

Manikavasagar's service to Lord Shiva contined. One day Lord Shiva wanted to bless the saint. Shiva asked Manikavasagar to sing the complete "Thiruvasagam" which he had composed. Lord wrote them down and also asked him to sing hyms in praise of the Dancing Lord of Thillai as a hero. Lord Shiva wrote them in the palm leaves. The Lord affixed his seal as Manikavasagar. He left the palm leaves at the prakara steps of the temple and disappeared.

The next day the priests of Thilai were stunned to find the scripture on the steps with the Lord's signature. The priests rushed to Manikavasagar and appraised him about it. They wanted the saint to explain the importance and philosophical terms of the compositions.

Manikavasagar took them to a golden hall abode of the Lord and showed them the Dancing Lord and said that he is is the meanig of what he wrote. Then, he immersed and became one with the almighty.

Manikavasagar Temple

Chidambaram temple

65

SEKKIZHAR

Sekkizhar was born in a Tondaimandalam Mudaliar family as Arulmozhithevan. He was a native of Kundrathur village (near Chennai). Kundrathur was a part of Puliyarkottam in Thondaimandalam. Sekkizhar was a child prodigy. He showed exemplary qualities as he grew up.

Kulothunga Chola II appointed him as his prime minister on account of his brilliance. Sekkizhar was well versed in both the Vedas and Agamas. Being a Saivite, he gained great knowledge about Nayanars-the ardent Shiva devotees. He compiled and wrote Periyapuranam or the great narrative about the lives of the sixty three Nayanmars. He sang the compilation in the Thousand Pillared Hall of Chidambaram temple.

Thousand pillared mandapam, Nataraja temple, Chidambaram

According to a legend, when Sekkizhar sat puzzled and pondered how to begin his work, Lord Shiva appeared and said his first verse should be: Ulakalam.

King Kulathunga Chola II was stunned and impressed by the great work of Sekkizhar. He placed the poem and Sekkizhar on the royal elephant and took them out on a grand procession around the streets of Chidambaram. The king himself waved the fly-whisks and showered the scholar with honors. The Periyapurnam is considered a fifth Veda and took its place as the twelfth and the last book in the Saiva canon.

Sekkizhar temple, Kundrathur

66

CAUVERY (KAVERI) RIVER

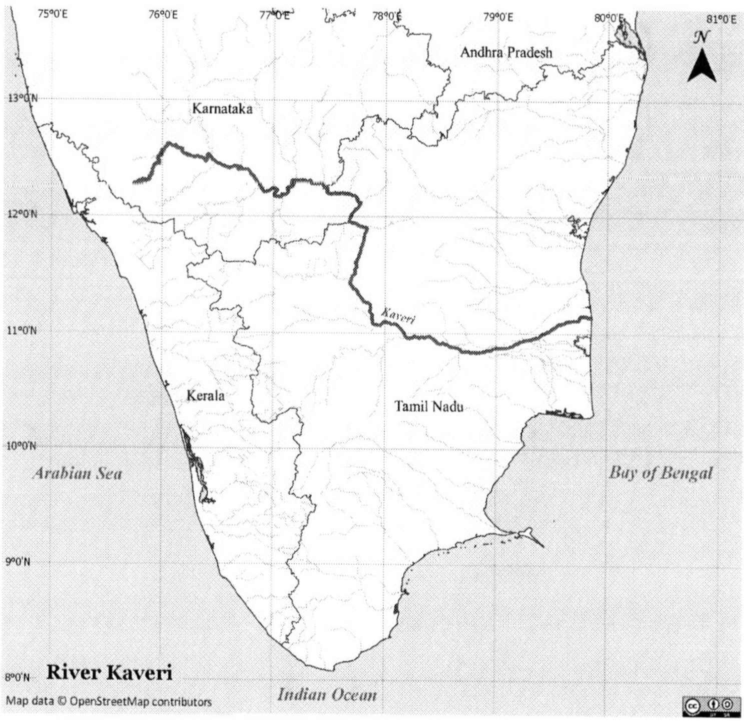

The Cauvery (Kaveri) river is the fourth largest river in India. It is called "Ponni" in Tamil. The river has its origin in the Western Ghats at Talakaveri. The river flows through

Karnataka and Tamil Nadu. It finally flows into the Bay of Bengal at Poompuhar, also known as Kaveripoompattinam.

The total river length is 802 kilometers from source to mouth. The stretch is one of the most fertile regions in India. The major tributaries, Kabini and Moyar join it before it reaches Mettur in Tamil Nadu.

The Cauvery is a celebrated waterbody in TamilNadu. People of Tamil Nadu worship the river for health, peace and prosperity. There are more than 500 Hindu temples located in the river banks. The significance of the river is elaborated in Tamil literature from the Sangam era (5th BCE to 3rd Centuiry CE). The "Pattina Palai" a Tamil poetic work duing the Sangam period speaks about Cauveri.

A Sanskrit sloka in praise of Cauvery

मारुद्धृते महाभागे महादेवि मनोहरे।
सर्वाभीष्टप्रदे देवि स्त्रास्थितां पुण्यवर्धिनि। ।1 । ।
सर्वपापक्षयकरे मम पापं विनाशय।
कवेरकन्ये कावेरि समुद्रमहिषिप्रिये। ।2 । ।
देहि मे भक्तिमुक्ति त्वं सर्वतीर्थस्वरूपिणि।
सिन्धुवर्ये दयासिन्धो मामुद्धर दयांबुधे। ।3 । ।
स्त्रियं देहि सुतं देहि श्रियं देहि ततः स्वगा।
आयुष्यं देहि चारोग्यं ऋणान्मुक्तं कुरुष्व माम्। ।माम्4 । ।
तासां च सरितां मध्ये सह्यकन्याघनाशिनि।
कावेरि लोकविख्याता जनतापनिवारिणि। ।5 । ।
इति ब्रह्माण्ड पुराणे कावरी प्रार्थना। ।

The Tamil literatures like Purananooru and Puranaraatru Padai have reference about the grandeur and its usefulness to vast stretches of lands. In Kamba Ramayanam, Kambar refers to it, making a comparison of the Kosala Kingdom of Sri Rama with the sovereignty of the Cholas. He attributes the flourishing Chola Kingdom to the perennial river Cauvery. The five great epics of

Tamil literature like Silappatikaram, Manimekalai, Seeva Chinthamani, Valayapathi and Kundalakesi mention the divinity and resourcefulness of the river.

About 2000 years back, Chola King Karikalan built a stone dam across Cauvery in response to the farmers request for a dam to improve their paddy cultivation. The dam was called the "Grand Anaicut" by Sir Arthur Thomas Cotton, a renowned British engineer.

Among the 500 plus temples built alongthe course of Cauvery, three are most famous and visited by thousands of devotees and foreigners every year.The three temples:

1. Sri.Ranganatha Swami Temple,Sri Rangam
2. Brihadeeswara Temple. Tanjore
3. Sri Nataraja Temple, Chidambaram

Sri Rangam Temple

Thanjavur Brihadeeswara temple

Sri Nataraja Temple, Chidambaram

Legend

Apart from Tamil literature and verses, many legends exist about River Cauvery. According to Skanda Purana, the river flowed in Kailasa, the abode of Lord Shiva. Lord Shiva asked Cauvery (Kaveri) to enter sage Agastya's kamandalu so that he had a perpetual souce of water.

Sage Agastya crossed the Vindhyaas and came down south. In that era, the South was reeling under a severe draught.This peril happened because an asura had blocked the dark clouds that give copious rain. Seeing the situation of water starved south, he made an appeal to Lord Ganesa to solve the problem. Ganesa took wings as a crow and knocked down Agastya's Kamandalu.The release of water gushed through the south as Cauveri.

Abbey fallas : close to the sourc of the river Cauvery(kaveri)

67

COSMIC DANCE: A UNION OF ART, SCIENCE AND SPIRITUALITY

The rise in need to understand the movement in stillness and the stillness in movement.

"Hundreds of years ago, Indian artists created visual images of dancing Shiva in a beautiful series of bronzes. In our time, physicists have used the most advanced technology to portray the patterns of the cosmic dance. The metaphor of the cosmic dance thus unifies ancient mythology, religious art and modern physics."

–Fritjof Capra

Today, right at the click of a button we have the accessibility and the ease to learn various art forms even while being miles away from a teacher. Dance is one such art form which has gained immense popularity in the recent times. Even the classical dance forms are learnt in haste with an intention to be recognized as a "know it all" person with social media platforms coming to their aid for promoting themselves. While there is no harm for the artists or learners to use social media platforms as a tool to take the art form to wider audiences, it is only when they deviate from propagating the core essence of dance, that the art form loses its value.

Understanding the History

Indian performing arts dates back to the Vedic times mirroring the cosmic creation in various ways and forms. Especially dance holds a unique place as it is believed that dance or *NatyaVeda* (as said in Sanskrit), was created as the fifth *Veda* by Lord Brahma in order to make the essence of four prime Vedas- Rig, Yajur, Sama and Atharvana in a most accessible and comprehensible form. So essentially, *Natya Veda* was an amalgam of intellectual content from *Rig Veda*, the essence of music from *Saama Veda*, the mimetic art (*abhinayas*) from *Yajur Veda* and the emotional content (*rasas*) from the *Atharvana Veda*. *Naatya Veda* was the gateway to spiritual knowledge for a common man.

Cosmic Dancer - Lord Nataraja

Nataraja, the divine depiction of the Hindu God Shiva as dancer, is a symbolism for cosmic creation. While superficially dance is seen as movement or a form of exercise, the underlying essence of dance comes out only when it's viewed in sync with the movement or energy that holds the universe together. Dance form in its purity can be equated to what we call as fractals in Mathematics. Fractals are infinitely complex patterns which when observed closely can be found as self-similar across various scales. Just like fractals, the dance form from the Vedic ages can be seen as a similar depiction of the cosmic movement in a smaller, comprehensible scale as cosmic dance.

The Cosmic Dance of Lord Shiva Nataraja

Cosmic Dance

In Hinduism, Lord Shiva is considered the Supreme God of Time known as the God of Destroyer who destroys the cycle of time. While destroyer identity may sound negative, it is a positive aspect as it is only His benevolence that can destroy our ignorance and free us from the birth cycle. Nataraja, the dancing form of Lord Shiva, is the one who sweeps away illusion and ignorance with his dance.

The movements of atoms in the Universe

The dance of Nataraja is called as cosmic dance for a reason. It symbolizes the divine interplay of dynamic and static energy flow and not any random movement. It is a symbolism of cosmic cycles of construction and destruction. Also it represents the daily rhythm of birth and death which gets us to the point that every breath is a dance of the divine. But how much aware are we of the significance of the dance of our lives?

It is always fascinating to know how our Indian ancestors had the knowledge of cosmos. They went on to symbolize and intersperse it in the way of living in the form of culture, arts and scriptures so that the common man too had access to the divine knowledge. Nataraja is a clear depiction of one such ancestral knowledge passed on to the common man to experience and evolve.

Uniqueness of Nataraja's Form

To have a clear understanding, let us see how the form of the cosmic dancer, Nataraja embodies knowledge of the cosmos, something that even scientists find incomprehensible even after decades of research and analysis. The Vedic scriptures proclaim that the birth of the universe, its maintenance, destruction, the soul's obscuration and liberation are the five acts of His cosmic dance. Let us look into His form to understand the cosmic symbolization:

1. The first thing that meets our eyes is the circular arch of flames in which we find him dancing. It makes us wonder what is the need for a circular arch encompassing while the dance posture alone might suffice. But this is where the cosmos connection is significantly seen making this a divine interpretation. The cyclically closed arch symbolises the cosmic fire in Hinduism- the fire that creates and consumes everything. It represents the cycle of life, of breath and death.
2. The locks in His hair interspersed with flowers, a skull, crescent moon and the figure of Ganga. The skull stands as a symbol of mortality, the personified image of Ganga depicts fertility. The crescent in His tuft depicts the cycle of time.
3. When it comes to ornamentation, one ear of Nataraja has a male earring while the other has female earring representing the fusion of male and female qualities.
4. The face shows two eyes plus a slightly open thrid eye on His forehead, a symbolisation of equilibrium of the three *Gunas*: *Sattva, Rajas and Tamas*.
5. In His upper right hand He holds the *damru*, a small hourglass shaped drum that symbolises rhythm and time.
6. His upper left hand contains *Agni,* the cosmic fire that creates and consumes everything.

7. The lower right hand shows an *Abhaya Mudra*(gesture for fearlessness) which suggests that His devotees be fearless and just follow their *dharma*, righteousness.
8. The lower left hand bent downwards at the wrist pointing towards the raised foot symbolises upliftment and salvation to those who seek Him.
9. The cobra swirling around His waist depicts the *kundalini,* a coiling power innate in every being.
10. The dwarf upon which Lord Natraja dances is a symbol of ego and ignorance in an individual.
11. His legs are bent and the tufts of His hair are seen loose and flying out in thin strands during the dance which brings out the passion and high energy level at which which He dances.
12. Interestingly, in spite of all the varying and conflicting gestures and depiction of highly energetic and passionate dance, His facial expression can be seen to be stoic representing His calmness despite being immersed in contrasting forces; a symbol of meditation.

On the whole Lord Nataraja is a symbolization of the macrocosm.

Cosmic Dance in Subatomic Particles

The current education system views arts, science and spirituality as different streams while the ancestral wisdom actually finds all the fields of knowledge interlinked with spirituality as the common thread of connection. To understand how arts, science and spirituality is interlinked, the metaphor drawn between cosmic dance of Nataraja and the dance of sub atomic particles gives us a clear picture.

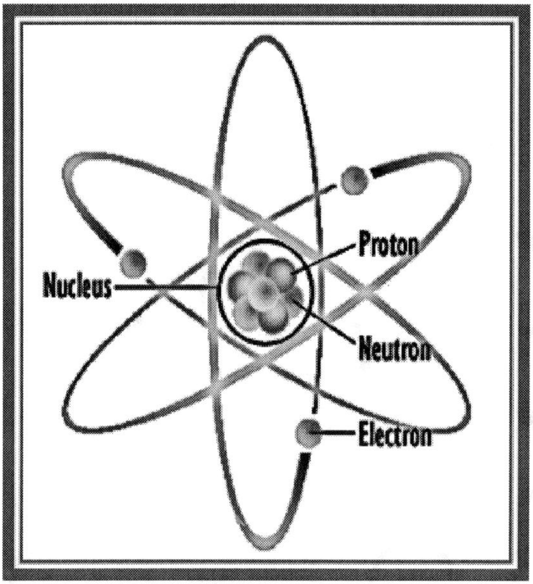

Tracing the path of movement of subatomic particles inside an atom.

As we know, atoms are the smallest unit of matter, the fundamental chemical element that constitutes the basis of everything in this Universe. Inside the atoms, we find the nucleus contains two types of subatomic particles, protons and neutrons. While the protons have positive electric charge, the neutrons have no electric charge. A third type of subatomic particle, electrons, move around the nucleus and are negatively charged.

In particle physics, it is found that there is a spinning movement inside the atom which traces the path as shown above and also without this movement there is no atom at all. So, if there is no subatomic movement, the existence of atom is null which in turn implies there is no existence of life too. This subatomic movement is only symbolized in the cosmic dance of Nataraja.

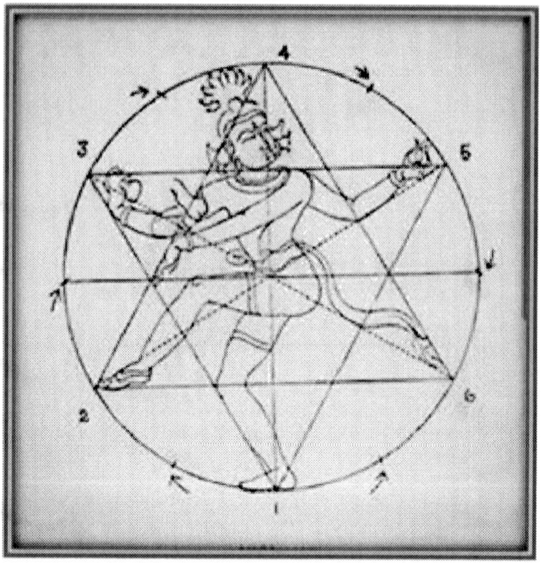

Lord Natraja's image symbolize the shape of subatomic particles movement inside an atom

It only makes sense to see how the macrocosm and microcosm are all nothing but movement of energies and how the Indian dance forms have captured its essence in its symbolization and movements.

Lord Nataraja statue at CERN (European Center of Nuclear Research)

While there are many a time where the ancestral wisdom derived from *Sanatana Dharma* (Hinduism) is overlooked or denied any importance calling it superstitious, we must understand that many such denials are deep rooted in political motives. What took the scientists decades of research and failures have already been laid down in Indian scriptures and practiced as a way of living.

Statue of Lord Nataraja at CERN

Even in the recent past, on June 18, 2004, when a 2m tall statue of the Indian deity Nataraja, the Lord of Dance was gifted to CERN, the European Center for Research in Particle Physics in Geneva, by the Indian government to celebrate the long association with the research center, many out rightly denied the significance of the choice of Lord Shiva Nataraja as a metaphor drawn to the dance of the subatomic particles. But apparently, one can't deny the fact on the placement a special plaque next to the Nataraja statue at CERN which is inscribed with many quotations from the renowned scientist Fritjof Capra's bestseller book *The Tao of Physics*. The text of the plaque reads:

Ananda K. Coomaraswamy, seeing beyond the unsurpassed rhythm, beauty, power and grace of Nataraja, once wrote of it "It is the clearest image of the activity of God which any art or religion can boast of."

More recently, Fritjof Capra explained that "Modern physics has shown that the rhythm of creation and destruction is not only manifest in the turn of the seasons and in the birth anddeath of all living creatures, but is also the very essence of inorganic matter," and that "for the modern physicists, the, Shiva's dance is the dance of subatomic matter."

It is indeed as Capra concluded: "Hundreds of years ago, Indian artists created visual images of dancing Shivas in a beautiful series of bronzes. In our time, physicists have used the most advanced technology to portray the patterns of the cosmic dance. The metaphor of the cosmic dance thus unifies ancient mythology, religious art and modern physics."

It is important for us to understand that what took scientists decades to observe, understand and prove has already been imparted through Vedic wisdom in various forms and modes. So it would only be wise for us to delve deep into the spiritual aspects of life and give it due importance and seek truth even while following a scientific course of experimentation.

The sacred secrets in store at Chidambaram

Having seen the metaphoric relation between the dance of Lord Nataraja and the movement of subatomic particles, it is important for us to look into the place, Chidambaram, where the famous Nataraja Temple is located before we move on to understand the significance of dance in cosmic connections above any other art forms.

The Chidambaram temple, TamilNadu, India

Chidambaram, where the famous Nataraja Temple is located, is in Tamil Nadu, India. What makes this place more significant and relevant to the topics we discussed above is that the temple here is built to mainly assist the spiritual journey of those who seek it. Firstly, it is located where the magnetic equator passes, which means the magnetic dip is zero at this location. Now how this assists in spiritual upliftment is, since the magnetic influence is negligible here, we are free from the Earth's magnetic field which is the last thing to pull down our physical dimension. Also, it is located 11-degree latitude and the centrifugal force (the outward force of the spinning Earth) is directly upward here. So, this helps to channelize our energies upward which assist in the awakening of the kundalini energy (an innate coiling power in every being).

Karanas of the Eastern Gopuram of Chidambaram temple

Furthermore, when we look into *Bharata's Natya Shastra*, the most ancient text on the performing arts composed by sage Bharata, we learn about *Karanas*. *Karana* is nothing but the coordinated action of body, the hands and the feet. There are 108 such *karanas* which are named and defined in Natya Shastra. Now, what is awe inspiring is, Chidambaram Nataraja Temple is the only place where we find all the 108 *karanas* as in Natya Shastra, depicted in the sculptures of the temple. While there are *karanas* found in other famous temples like *Rajarajeshwara* temple in Tanjore, the *Sarangapani* temple in Kumbakonam, the *Arunachaleshwara* temple in Thiruvannamalai and *Vriddhagirishvara* temple in Vriddhachalam, it's only in Chidambaram that we find all 108 *karanas* depicted. This uniqueness makes the place more significant and makes us marvel at the mysticism the place holds.

Here, there arises a question as why specifically 108 *karanas* was mentioned in texts and depicted in sculptures. What's the significance of the number 108? This question leads me to the point where the number 9 is considered as a cosmic number. As per numerology, the sum of digits in 108 leads to the cosmic number 9. So, is there any relationship between the 108 karanas and the cosmic connection?

Interestingly we can find the significance of number 108 in various aspects of Hinduism like there are 108 Upanishads, 108 *Marmas* with regard to *Ayurveda*, 108 names for each deity in Hinduism, 108 beads in a *Japa Mala,* etc. When it comes to cosmic relations, the ancient Indian concepts of astronomy found that the average distance of the Sun and the Moon to Earth is 108 times their respective diameters. So does the cyclic movement of sun and moon around the earth have anything of relevance to the 108 *karanas*? Well, as we ruminate over the above concepts and questions, let's us get back to where we started, cosmic dance, the union of art, science and spirituality. Now why is it that it is called as Cosmic dance and not as Cosmic art or Cosmic painting or Cosmic singing?

The relevance of dance in spirituality

In Vedic scriptures there is this *vaakya* which goes *"Geetam vaadyam tatha nrityam sangitam uchyate"*. It translates to defining three-fold nature of music as union of sound, rhythm and movement. And one can easily see that dance is the only art form where one can find all the three aspects. Again, this relationship between sound, rhythm and movement can be found to have cosmic connection.

The analogy between the dynamic Universal energy and the cosmic dance can be traced by considering the following points:

1. The fundamental sounds in existence are 'aaa', 'ouuu' and 'mmm' which when uttered together sounds as AUM which is found to be the universal sound.
2. The basic cosmic rhythms that subtly guide our body are daily rhythms, tidal rhythms, monthly or lunar rhythms and annual or seasonal rhythms.
3. The dance in universe can be seen in the movement of subatomic particles as discussed before.

Thus, the above three aspects of universal sound, rhythm and dance can be compared to the *raagas*/music, 108 *talas*/beats and 108 *karanas*(movements) while performing dance which makes our point of dance being called as cosmic dance stronger.

We can also view it this way. Let's take the case of a painting or singing. We can have a painting in a canvas and a song recorded in a cassette. In both cases, we can view/ hear the art form separated from the artist. While with dance, as an art form, dance can never be separated from the dancer just like how we cannot separate our breath and air. The whole Universe can be viewed as a manifestation of an energy form, which scientifically can neither be destroyed nor created. Similarly, dance in its purest form can be viewed as one with the cosmic movement. This is the essence of dance that has its origin in ancient Indian scriptures.

Cosmic Dance of Life

The main objective of writing this article was to bring

awareness among learners of classical dance, forms of the essence it holds. As mentioned at the start of the article, in this era of social media influence, art forms are losing their lustre as they are mostly practiced and promoted in commercial interests. In modern times, dance is perceived as mere stage performances, the display of artistry and performer's mastery over dance. We must understand that the classical dance forms are deep rooted in the Indian Vedic scriptures which had its motive rooted in spirituality.

Essentially a good dance performance should evoke the *rasa* of being in one with the Supreme to its audience. And that would happen only when the dancer loses themselves in the dance, a significant moment of one's destruction of ego.

Finding Purpose

It's vital to know the purpose of life to understand the importance of cosmic dance. While the materialistic world that we breathe in can make us comprehend the purpose of life as being healthy, wealthy, famous, happy and successful with vast material possessions, the actual purpose of life can be totally contradicting. The actual purpose of life as per *Sanatana Dharma*, is to realize the Supreme and become one with Him, breaking free from the birth-death cycle, called *Moksha* (salvation).

One may ask how is cosmic dance relevant to salvation. Well, all the topics covered here are just a brief outline of a profound ocean of Vedic wisdom.

Let me try to put it in simpler terms. Firstly, every being is born with the innate power called the kundalini power which lies coiled around our waist. We must understand that we are ignorant and believe that we are limited to our body and all attempts of our ancestral wisdom to help us awaken the innate power and realize a higher level of consciousness has not happened. We have to transcend the boundaries of our body consciousness and that wouldn't happen till we are struck running after wealth, fame, physique and other materialistic needs.

The way forward

First and foremost, have faith in the ancient Indian Vedic values. To be clear, I'm not talking about the religious dogma that keeps changing over time but the spiritual values of *Sanathana Dharma* that is rooted in eternal truth. Even a trained physicist Fritjof Capra, who spent 20 years from 1965-85 in doing research in theoretical high energy physics, draws the parallel between science and spirituality. As a person who developed deep interest in Eastern spiritual traditions, he says, the practice of meditation helped him experienced a strong sense of empowerment. In fact, he says it was an experience of epiphany that led him to the writing of the book 'The Tao of Physics' that draws connection between Lord Nataraja's cosmic dance and the dance in subatomic particles. Here is what he has to say about his epiphany in his own words (taken from Mystics and Scientists in the Twenty-First Century: Science and Spirituality Revisited by Fritjof Capra- 40th Anniversary Mystics and Scientists Conference Horsley Park, Surrey, 7-9 April, 2017):

I was sitting by the ocean one late summer afternoon, watching the waves rolling in and feeling the rhythm of my breathing, when I suddenly became aware of my whole environment as being engaged in a gigantic cosmic dance. Being a physicist, I knew that the sand, rocks, water, and air around me were made of vibrating molecules and atoms, and that these consisted of particles which interacted with one another by creating and destroying other particles. I knew also that the Earth's atmosphere was continually bombarded by showers of so-called "cosmic rays" — particles of high energy undergoing multiple collisions as they penetrate the air. All this was familiar to me from my research in high-energy physics, but until that moment I had only experienced it through graphs, diagrams, and mathematical theories. As I sat on that beach in meditation, my former experiences came to life. I "saw" cascades of energy coming down from outer space, in which particles were created and destroyed in rhythmic pulses. I "saw" the atoms of the elements and those of my body participating in this cosmic dance of energy. I felt its rhythm and I "heard" its sound; and that moment I knew that this was the Dance of Shiva, the Lord of Dancers worshipped in Hinduism.

As we could see, a Western Scientist gains the mystic knowledge of the cosmos while he was meditative. He had faith in the Eastern spiritual tradition and followed it. So this belief in the Vedic tradition is the foundation step for our way forward.

Meditation and Cosmic Dance

Now that we know spiritual progress is the only way forward towards realizing the purpose of our life, let us see how we can start with it. As per Vedic teachings, meditation is the ultimate way to realizing the Supreme and since the universal divine Self dwells within the heart, the way to experience and recognize the Supreme is by turning one's attention inward in a process of contemplative meditation. While one may think that meditation and cosmic dance portray the opposites, stillness and movement, it's actually wrong. If we see dance as just movement of body, a way of exercise or view it just for its aesthetics, we may not find the connection between meditation and cosmic dance.

Let us look at it this way. There are various kinds of movements happening at different scales both inside and outside our body. You may agree that the breath of life, the *prana,* is the connecting force between us and the cosmos. Now, meditation is about turning our attention inward to experience this *pranashakthi*. As we keep contemplating, over time, even while we dance, our body, mind and soul is all turned inward where we get to experience moments of heightened aliveness. Spiritual experience comes in those moments of heightened aliveness of mind and body as a unity. It is this unity that one can experience through cosmic dance which is symbolically represented by the Lord Nataraja.

Learning and practicing dance knowing its underlying Vedic essence can help us evolve spiritually. And with spiritual growth, one can experience movement in stillness and stillness in movement. Also, it would no more make sense to view arts, science and spirituality as difference streams of knowledge.

To the rhythm of waves,
Sound of the cosmos,
Dance in tune to your breath
Prana, the essence of life
Will hold you together
In body, mind and soul
As one with the Supreme.